BEHIND THE COUNTER

EVOLUTION OF INDIAN PHARMA RETAIL

SUJIT PAUL

notionpress.com

INDIA • SINGAPORE • MALAYSIA

ISBN

Hardcase 979-8-90560-820-9
Paperback 979-8-90560-459-1

Preface

India's pharmacy retail landscape is undergoing a seismic shift—one that's rewriting the rules of access, affordability, and accountability in healthcare. From small neighborhood chemists to organized pharmacy chains, from mom-and-pop stores to tech-enabled platforms, the pharmacy ecosystem is rapidly evolving to meet the demands of a growing, diverse, and health-conscious population.

This book was born out of a simple question: *How did we get here, and where are we headed?*

Why This Book?

Because the pharmacy retail sector in India is not just about dispensing medicine—it is the frontline of healthcare for millions. Yet, it remains under-documented, misunderstood, and often overlooked in broader conversations about healthcare innovation. This book aims to spotlight the evolution, challenges, and triumphs of this dynamic sector while offering a blueprint for what the future may hold.

We explore how traditional models have morphed into modern chains, how technology is reshaping consumer behavior, how regulatory frameworks are catching up, and how players—big and small—are navigating a space that is equal parts opportunity and complexity.

Who is This Book For?

- **Entrepreneurs and business leaders** exploring or operating in the healthcare, pharma, or retail domains.
- **Investors and analysts** looking to decode the potential and patterns of India's pharmacy boom.
- **Academicians, students, and researchers** seeking a comprehensive understanding of India's healthcare retail infrastructure.
- **Policy-makers and regulators** interested in insights that blend ground realities with industry aspirations.
- And **curious minds** who believe that a healthy nation is built not just in hospitals—but in the everyday conversations between pharmacists and people.

What Can You Expect to Gain?

This book offers more than just a chronology of events—it is a **lens**, a **map**, and a **mirror**.

- A **lens** to observe the micro and macro trends shaping pharmacy retail in India.
- A **map** to navigate business models, supply chain innovations, digital disruptions, and market dynamics.
- A **mirror** reflecting the voices of those on the ground—pharmacists, retailers, consumers, and thought leaders.

We invite you to journey with us through stories of resilience, data-backed analysis, and forward-thinking perspectives. Whether you're building a startup, shaping policy, or simply curious about the invisible lifeline that sustains Indian healthcare—this book is for you.

Table of Contents

Preface .... *iii*

Chapter 1 Introduction to Pharma Retail 1
Chapter 2 Regulatory and Compliance Framework 10
Chapter 3 Role of Key Stakeholders.. 25
Chapter 4 Business Models in Pharma Retail........................... 39
Chapter 5 Location, Store Design & Inventory Planning......... 49
Chapter 6 Procurement & Vendor Management....................... 59
Chapter 7 Hiring and Training Pharmacists & Staff................ 69
Chapter 8 Technology and Automation in Retail Pharmacy..... 82
Chapter 9 Store Operations and Standard Operating Procedures 92
Chapter 10 Marketing in Pharma Retail 103
Chapter 11 E-commerce & Omnichannel Strategy 122
Chapter 12 Expanding the Chain 139
Chapter 13 Seasonal and Emergency Demand Management.. 149
Chapter 14 Managing Expiry and Returns 158
Chapter 15 Ethical Selling and Pharmacy Code of Conduct 170

Appendix A: Checklists *181*
Appendix B: Sample Forms and Templates *185*
Acknowledgments.. *187*
About the Author *189*

Chapter 1

Introduction to Pharma Retail

The story of pharmaceutical retail is, in many ways, a mirror of our broader social and technological progress. What began as small, community-based apothecaries serving a local clientele has evolved into a sophisticated, tech-enabled network of health service providers that operate at the intersection of medicine, commerce, and public health. Over the last century, the role of the pharmacist and the retail pharmacy has undergone dramatic shifts, not just in the products they dispense, but in the very purpose they serve within society. This evolution has been shaped by a combination of factors: advances in pharmaceutical manufacturing, changing healthcare policies, shifts in consumer behavior, and the integration of technology into nearly every aspect of our lives.

In the early 20th century, pharmacies were far more than just places to fill prescriptions. They were community gathering points, often equipped with soda fountains and counters serving ice cream sundaes, malts, and fizzy beverages. It could be referred to as the Soda Fountain Era (1920–1949) of pharma retail.

Pharmacists dispensed medicines, yes. But they also sold cosmetics, tobacco, newspapers, and an array of household goods. This was the age when the local druggist was both a healthcare provider and a neighborhood personality, knowing customers by name and often offering informal advice. With compounding still a routine task, pharmacists would measure, grind, and mix ingredients on the spot, blending science with a certain old-world charm.

Around 1950–1979, the post-war boom brought mass production to pharmaceuticals. Large-scale manufacturing by drug companies greatly reduced the need for pharmacists to compound medicines in-house. Instead, their daily work shifted to tasks humorously summarized as "lick, stick, and pour"; lick the envelope for tablets, stick labels onto bottles, and pour pre-made liquid formulations. Pharmacies became more transactional, with less emphasis on personalized preparation and more on retail efficiency. Drugstore chains began to expand, bringing standardized branding and layouts. The role of the pharmacist, while still respected, became more narrowly focused on the physical act of dispensing, as opposed to advising or diagnosing.

By the late 20th century, a quiet revolution began in pharmacy practice. Rising healthcare costs, an aging population, and the increasing complexity of drug therapies spurred the profession to adopt a patient-centered model. Pharmacists became active participants in care, offering medication counseling, checking for drug interactions, and helping patients understand the importance of adherence. Concepts like "medication therapy management" took hold, and many states expanded pharmacists' authority to provide certain vaccinations and conduct health screenings. Pharmacies began incorporating private consultation areas, signaling a shift from purely retail spaces to hybrid health service centers.

The last decade has brought unprecedented integration of pharmacy services into the wider healthcare ecosystem. Pharmacists now work closely with physicians, nurses, and other professionals in collaborative care models. The modern pharmacy offers far more than prescriptions, walk-in immunizations, chronic disease monitoring, travel health consultations, and even telehealth services are now common. Technology plays a central role, from automated dispensing systems to mobile apps for refills and medication reminders. This era also sees the rise of online and mail-order pharmacies, giving patients 24/7 access to medicines. With public health emergencies like the COVID-19 pandemic, pharmacists stepped to the front lines, administering millions of vaccines and providing vital community health services.

Today's pharmacy is as much a health destination as it is a retail store, blending clinical expertise, personalized care, and technological convenience. The journey from soda fountains to Artificial intelligence-powered prescription platforms reflects not only the evolution of a profession but also the changing ways society defines healthcare access and community wellness.

India's pharmaceutical retail story is a unique blend of policy-driven transformation, entrepreneurial ambition, and technological disruption. Unlike Western markets, where the sector's growth was largely fueled by corporate consolidation and insurance-linked healthcare, India's journey was profoundly shaped by its own socio-economic priorities and regulatory frameworks.

The way people in India buy medicines has changed a lot over the years. Back in the 1970s, a big policy change set the stage for today's industry. At that time, India decided that patents would only be given for the process of making a drug, not the final product itself. This meant Indian companies could legally make the same medicine using a different process, which opened the door for affordable "generic" drugs. This move helped India become known as the "pharmacy of the developing world" because it could make and export low-cost medicines to many countries.

Fast forward to 2008, when the government started the Jan Aushadhi Scheme (now called Pradhan Mantri Bhartiya Janaushadhi Pariyojana- PMBJP). The idea was simple: open special stores to sell affordable generic medicines so that even people in small towns could access them. Over the years, these stores have multiplied, with more than 10,000 outlets now running across the country.

Alongside government efforts, private pharmacy chains also began to grow. Apollo Pharmacy, which started in 1987, and MedPlus, launched in 2006, set a new standard for how a pharmacy looked and worked. These chains were not just shops for buying pills, they often had in-house diagnostics, loyalty programs, and even online ordering.

Then came the game-changer: e-pharmacies. Companies like PharmEasy, 1mg, and NetMeds brought the pharmacy to people's smartphones. Customers could upload prescriptions, get home delivery, enjoy discounts, and even consult doctors online. COVID-19 lockdowns supercharged this trend, making online medicine buying more common.

Today, e-pharmacies account for only about 1-3% of total medicine sales in India, but their growth has been rapid. However, the law is still catching up. In 2018, the government introduced Draft E-Pharmacy Rules to ensure these businesses have proper licenses, qualified pharmacists on duty, and strong data privacy protections for customers.

Now, India's pharma retail scene is a mix of brick-and-mortar stores and digital platforms. Whether it's walking into a local Jan Aushadhi outlet, visiting a well-known chain like Apollo, or ordering from an app like 1mg, people have more options than ever. The focus has shifted from simply selling medicines to offering complete healthcare solutions, from tests to consultations, making pharmacies an important part of India's healthcare system.

Overview of Indian and Global Pharmaceutical Retail Markets

The pharmaceutical retail market, essentially the bridge between drug manufacturers and everyday consumers, has become a cornerstone of the healthcare system worldwide. It spans everything from the small, friendly neighborhood chemist who knows his customers by name to sprawling pharmacy chains and digital-first platforms delivering medicines at lightning speed. While the industry serves the same ultimate goal everywhere, making medicines accessible, its size, structure, and growth patterns differ greatly between India and the rest of the world.

Globally, the pharmacy retail sector is estimated to be worth over USD 1.4 trillion in 2024, with steady growth driven by longer life spans, better healthcare access, and the rising burden of chronic diseases like diabetes, hypertension, and heart disease. North America, Europe, China, and Japan dominate the market, largely because of mature healthcare systems and higher per capita spending on medicines. In developed countries, large organized chains lead the way. In the United States, for instance, giants like Walgreens, CVS Health, and Walmart Pharmacy combine prescription sales with clinics, diagnostic services, and wellness products under one roof. In Europe, trusted names such as Boots in the UK, Apoteket in Sweden, and dm-drogerie markt in Germany operate within tightly regulated systems supported by strong health insurance coverage. Meanwhile, in Asia, players like Sinopharm in China and Tsuruha Holdings in Japan have rapidly expanded, blending physical retail with online ordering, home delivery, and increasingly, telemedicine. One major global shift in recent years has been the rise of "omnichannel healthcare," where offline pharmacies, online platforms, and virtual doctor consultations are seamlessly integrated, letting patients manage prescriptions, consultations, and medicine delivery from a single provider.

In contrast, India's pharmaceutical retail market is much younger but is expanding at one of the fastest rates in the world. Currently valued at around USD 20-25 billion, it is on track for significant growth fueled by a rapidly growing population, especially in urban areas, greater health awareness, expanding health insurance coverage, and government schemes aimed at making essential medicines more affordable. The market structure here is unique. The unorganized sector, consisting of roughly 8–9 lakh small, independent chemist shops, still accounts for the majority of sales, especially in smaller cities and rural belts. These outlets rely on close ties with local doctors and long-standing relationships with customers. On the other side, organized retail chains such as Apollo Pharmacy, MedPlus, Wellness Forever, and Guardian Pharmacy are bringing a more standardized approach, offering better inventory management, professional store layouts, and customer loyalty programs. E-pharmacies, including big names like PharmEasy, Tata 1mg, NetMeds, and Amazon Pharmacy, are growing rapidly but currently make up only about 1-3% of total sales, partly due to evolving regulations and consumer trust factors.

Compared to developed countries, where the market is consolidated and dominated by a few large chains, India remains highly fragmented. Regulatory frameworks abroad tend to be stricter, particularly around online medicine sales, while India is still refining its legal structure, with the Draft E-Pharmacy Rules awaiting finalization. Another major distinction is the role of pharmacists. In countries like the US, pharmacists often provide vaccinations, conduct health screenings, and help patients manage long-term conditions. In India, pharmacists' clinical involvement is still in its early stages, though it is likely to expand over time.

Whether in India or globally, pharmacy retail is moving towards a future where it is more than just a point of sale; it is an integral part of healthcare delivery. The pharmacy of tomorrow will not only dispense medicines but also act as a wellness hub, offering preventive care, basic diagnostic tests, pharmacist consultations, telemedicine, and access to health and nutrition products. With rapid advances in digital health, we can expect to see AI-enabled prescription tracking, improved supply chain transparency, and personalized medicine delivery becoming mainstream. Ultimately, the evolution of pharma retail reflects a larger shift in healthcare: from reactive treatment to proactive, patient-centered care.

If you walk through the bustling lanes of a small Indian town, chances are you'll spot a familiar neighbourhood chemist shop, the kind where the owner knows half the customers by name, remembers your usual prescription, and might even extend credit if you're short on cash. These are standalone pharmacies, the backbone of India's pharmaceutical retail for decades. Often run by individual pharmacists or family businesses, they thrive on personal relationships, trust, and local community presence. In emergencies, these stores are sometimes the first point of contact, offering quick, informal health advice and essential medicines at short notice.

However, standalone pharmacies operate on limited resources. Their purchasing power with suppliers is small, meaning they often can't offer deep discounts like larger players. Stock variety might be limited to the most essential or fast-moving medicines, and advanced systems for inventory management or digital billing are less common. Still, their strength lies in their adaptability and the deep-rooted trust they enjoy within their localities.

At the other end of the spectrum are chain pharmacies, sleek, uniform stores operating under the umbrella of a corporate brand. In India, names like Apollo Pharmacy, MedPlus, and Wellness Forever have become synonymous with professional service, consistent product availability, and the convenience of multiple outlets. Globally, giants such as CVS Health in the US, Boots in the UK, and Watsons across Asia dominate with large-scale operations. Chains enjoy bulk purchasing power, enabling them to offer competitive prices and a wider range of products, from prescription drugs to health supplements, personal care, and even in-store health services. Their use of technology, mobile apps, loyalty programs, and home delivery services caters well to the digital-savvy customer.

Looking ahead, the future of pharma retail in India is not about one model replacing the other, but about coexistence and convergence. Standalone pharmacies are increasingly exploring partnerships, franchise models, and group purchasing organisations to enjoy the economies of scale that chains offer. Meanwhile, chains are learning to localize their service, tailoring their approach to match the trust-based relationships that independent chemists have cultivated for generations. Globally, the trend is leaning towards hybrid models that integrate physical stores with strong online platforms, ensuring customers can get medicines when and how they need them.

References

- https://www.mdpi.com/500168
- Wikipedia – History of pharmacy in the United States
- Emporos – Pharmacy Commerce Timeline
- Wikipedia – Pharmacy Automation
- Pharmacy Times – The Pharmacy Industry Then and Now
- Commonwealth Fund – Competition, Consolidation, and Evolution in the Pharmacy Market
- PharmaTutor – A Saga of 75 Years Journey of Indian Pharmaceutical Industry
- IBEF – Pharmaceuticals Industry Report
- Market Xcel – Omnichannel Trends in Pharmacy Retail
- Department of Pharmaceuticals – PMBJP
- Apollo Pharmacy Company Profile
- MedPlus Company Profile
- Draft E-Pharmacy Rules, 2018 – Government of India
- PharmEasy Company Overview
- India Brand Equity Foundation – Pharmaceuticals
- Statista – Global Retail Pharmacy Market Size
- IBEF – Pharmaceuticals Industry in India
- Mordor Intelligence – Indian Pharmacy Retail Market Report

- FICCI – E-Pharmacy Working Group Report
- WHO – Role of Pharmacists in Healthcare
- IBEF – Indian Pharmaceuticals Industry
- FICCI – Indian Pharmaceutical Retail Sector Report
- Statista – Global Pharmaceutical Retail Market

Chapter 2

Regulatory and Compliance Framework

Pharmaceutical retail in India is a sector where business and public health intersect in profound ways. Every action a pharmacy takes, from ordering stock to handling prescriptions to advising patients, has consequences that ripple through communities. Unlike many other commercial enterprises, pharmacy retail carries an inherent responsibility that blends legal obligation, professional ethics, and social accountability. The regulatory and compliance framework governing this sector is intricate, designed not to hinder business but to protect patients, ensure safe and effective medication distribution, and preserve public trust in the healthcare system. At first glance, the web of rules and guidelines may seem overwhelming, but a deeper look reveals a well-structured framework that balances flexibility with patient safety and professional integrity.

Overview of Indian Pharmacy Laws

The roots of regulatory oversight in Indian pharmacy retail stretch back more than seventy years. The Drugs and Cosmetics Act of 1940, alongside the Drugs and Cosmetics Rules of 1945, established the foundational principles governing the manufacture, sale, and distribution of medicines. Their core intent was to ensure that medicines reaching the public were safe, effective, and of consistent quality. Over the decades, these regulations evolved, adapting to new pharmaceutical technologies, changing therapeutic practices, and the expanding role of pharmacists in patient care. Today, regulatory responsibility is shared across several agencies. At the national level, the Central Drugs Standard Control Organization (CDSCO) oversees drug approvals, clinical trial regulations, and ensures uniform compliance. Complementing it, state drug authorities manage inspections, monitor licenses, and enforce local regulations. Agencies such as the Food Safety and Standards Authority of India (FSSAI) add another layer, regulating nutraceuticals and dietary supplements, reflecting the sector's growing diversification into preventive health.

Drug License (Forms 20/21, 20B/21B)

Licensing forms the cornerstone of regulatory compliance. No pharmacy can operate legally without the appropriate licenses, and these vary depending on the nature of the business. Retail pharmacies usually operate under Form 20, which permits them to dispense prescription drugs directly to patients. Wholesale licenses, used by businesses that supply medications to retailers, typically require Form 21. Specialized licenses, such as 20B and 21B, are needed for certain categories of drugs that carry higher risk, including potent antibiotics, controlled substances, and narcotics. Obtaining a license is a meticulous process. Regulatory authorities examine the physical premises, staff qualifications, storage facilities, and operational procedures. Inspections are sometimes conducted even before licenses are granted. Though procedural, this thorough scrutiny ensures a standard baseline of safety and quality across the pharmacy sector.

GST Implications for Pharmacy Retail

Beyond licensing, financial compliance adds another layer of operational responsibility. The Goods and Services Tax (GST) system, introduced in India in 2017, simplified taxation but introduced nuanced challenges for pharmacy operators. Medicines are classified into categories, with essential drugs often exempt and branded or specialty drugs subject to standard GST rates.

Multi-state pharmacies face the additional challenge of reconciling minor variations in tax procedures across states. Failure to correctly categorize drugs or file returns can result in penalties, delayed operations, or legal complications. To manage this, many pharmacies invest in integrated software solutions that handle billing, inventory, and tax filing simultaneously, reducing human error and ensuring smooth audits.

Understanding Schedule H, H1, and X Drugs: Handling and Documentation

A defining aspect of pharmaceutical compliance is the management of controlled and scheduled drugs. Indian law classifies medications based on their potential for misuse, therapeutic risks, and public health implications. Schedule H drugs require a valid prescription for dispensing. Schedule H1 drugs, which include certain antibiotics, steroids, and other high-risk formulations, mandate meticulous record-keeping in separate registers. Schedule X drugs, encompassing narcotics and psychotropic substances, demand the strictest security and documentation measures. Secure storage, transaction logs, and routine reporting to authorities are non-negotiable. For pharmacists, this is not merely a matter of legal compliance; it is a safeguard for patient safety. Mishandling or misdispensing such drugs can have life-altering consequences for patients, while also attracting severe penalties for the pharmacy.

The complexity of compliance grows exponentially for multi-state operations. While the basic licensing framework is central, states may introduce additional rules or interpret regulations differently. Storage temperature guidelines, documentation protocols, and inspection practices can vary from one state to another. Consider a pharmacy chain operating in Maharashtra, Karnataka, and Gujarat. Transporting a Schedule X drug between these states involves permits, adherence to security protocols, and accurate documentation for each batch. Staff training becomes essential, ensuring uniform compliance despite regional regulatory nuances. Companies often rely on centralized compliance teams, internal audits, and technology-driven tracking systems to manage this complexity. Real-world accounts from pharmacy chains highlight the importance of continuous training workshops and digital monitoring systems in maintaining regulatory consistency across multiple outlets.

Digital platforms add further layers of regulatory oversight. The rise of e-pharmacies such as PharmEasy, 1mg, NetMeds, and Amazon Pharmacy has transformed medicine access, enabling prescription uploads, doorstep delivery, and virtual consultations. Yet, these platforms are not exempt from regulatory scrutiny. They must maintain valid licenses, employ qualified pharmacists, secure patient data, and ensure every transaction complies with central and state laws. The Draft E-Pharmacy Rules of 2018 outline stringent guidelines to safeguard patient safety, maintain proper records, and ensure accountability. For operators, this integration of digital and physical compliance is an operational necessity, requiring robust workflows that track stock, patient interactions, prescriptions, and deliveries while maintaining legal transparency.

CDSCO, FSSAI, and State-Level Regulatory Agencies

Compliance is not solely about following rules; it is a daily operational challenge, particularly in high-volume environments. Take the example of a medium-sized chain handling thousands of prescriptions daily. Schedule H1 drugs require not only precise dispensing but also accurate record entry in dedicated registers. Any error, delay, or misplacement can trigger inspection flags, fines, or reputational damage. Successful pharmacies often report that staff training, clear workflows, and automated systems are the backbone of effective compliance. For instance, in some chains, digital systems automatically log H1 transactions, issue alerts for near-expiry drugs, and synchronize multi-location inventory to prevent shortages or overstocking.

Inspections are another critical aspect. Regulatory authorities can conduct routine or surprise visits, examining licenses, registers, storage, temperature logs, GST records, and patient transaction documentation. Pharmacies that maintain a culture of continuous compliance rarely encounter issues during inspections. In contrast, ad hoc or reactive approaches often lead to fines, temporary shutdowns, or prolonged audits. Interviews with pharmacists reveal that viewing compliance as a continuous process rather than a periodic obligation creates operational resilience and trust among staff, patients, and regulators alike.

Real-world anecdotes highlight the human dimension of compliance. One family-run pharmacy in a small town faced the challenge of expanding into a neighboring state. Each state had slightly different expectations for storage, temperature monitoring, and record-keeping. By leveraging digital registers, internal audits, and staff cross-training, they successfully navigated inspections in both states while maintaining uninterrupted patient service. Another chain integrated artificial intelligence to monitor expiry dates, cold chain adherence, and drug schedules, reducing manual errors and enhancing audit readiness. These examples illustrate that compliance is not only about legal adherence but also operational innovation, staff engagement, and patient safety.

The evolving role of pharmacists in regulatory compliance reflects a broader transformation in healthcare. Modern pharmacists are expected to manage operational details, advise patients, and monitor drug safety, all while adhering to stringent legal frameworks. This dual responsibility requires professional rigor, ongoing education, and a deep understanding of the ethical dimensions of pharmacy practice. Pharmacists often act as the first line of defense against medication errors, adverse reactions, and misuse. In India, where pharmacists are often the most accessible healthcare professionals, this role is amplified. Regulatory adherence ensures that pharmacists can perform these duties safely, confidently, and with the authority that patients and authorities trust.

Compliance extends beyond internal operations to interactions with manufacturers, distributors, and other stakeholders. Accurate invoicing, batch tracking, temperature monitoring during transportation, and timely reporting of adverse drug reactions are integral. Digital systems now allow real-time tracking of shipments, automated alerts for storage deviations, and centralized reporting for multi-location operators. These tools enhance transparency, reduce human error, and support regulatory audits. In practice, pharmacies that invest in such systems often report smoother inspections, improved operational efficiency, and higher patient confidence.

India's regulatory framework is dynamic, continually adapting to new challenges. Novel drug formulations, complex biologics, and advanced delivery mechanisms demand updated storage, handling, and documentation practices. Digital health innovations, including telemedicine, e-prescriptions, and app-based consultations, necessitate regulatory agility. Pharmacovigilance systems monitor adverse events, providing alerts and updates that pharmacies must integrate promptly. Staying current is not optional; it requires active participation in professional associations, continuous learning, and engagement with regulatory bodies. For pharmacists, this ongoing commitment to knowledge and practice is both a professional obligation and a moral imperative.

Despite its complexity, the regulatory framework is ultimately protective. It ensures patient safety, operational transparency, and public trust. Compliance safeguards the pharmacy, enhances professional credibility, and protects patients from harm. Observing these regulations fosters a culture of responsibility that permeates every aspect of pharmacy operations, from stock management to patient interactions. In India, where pharmacies often function as community health touchpoints, this trust is invaluable. Patients rely on pharmacists for advice, support, and continuity of care. Regulatory adherence underpins this trust, ensuring that every transaction aligns with professional and legal standards.

Pharmacies also operate in a sphere where public awareness and behavior directly influence regulatory enforcement. Prescription misuse is a persistent concern in India. Many patients, especially in smaller towns and underserved areas, seek medications without proper prescriptions due to habit, convenience, or limited access to physicians. Pharmacists often find themselves in difficult positions, balancing empathy for the patient's situation with legal responsibilities. Regulatory frameworks establish clear boundaries, but real-world circumstances test these boundaries constantly. A pharmacist who refuses a Schedule H drug without a prescription may face confrontation or lose business to a less compliant competitor. Yet, choosing compliance reinforces long-term trust and protects the pharmacy from operational and legal risks. Over time, consistent adherence shapes healthier patient behavior and strengthens professional authority in the community.

The regulatory environment also emphasizes drug quality verification. Substandard and counterfeit medicines remain a challenge in parts of India's fragmented supply chain. Pharmacies are expected to maintain relationships with licensed and reputable distributors, verify product authenticity, and ensure proper documentation for every received batch. Regulatory vigilance, supported by supply chain digitization such as barcoding and batch authentication systems, serves as a critical defense against counterfeit drugs entering the market. When pharmacies prioritize trusted sourcing, they uphold patient safety even if operational costs rise marginally.

Storage, Temperature, and Labeling Compliance

Storage, temperature control, and labeling are other critical compliance dimensions. Many medicines, particularly vaccines, insulin, and certain biologics, are highly sensitive to temperature fluctuations. Cold-chain compliance is non-negotiable. Pharmacies maintain continuous temperature logs, implement fail-safe monitoring systems, and develop contingency plans for equipment malfunctions. Labels are equally vital. Each must clearly communicate drug strength, batch number, manufacturing and expiry dates, storage instructions, and specific warnings. These details might appear procedural, but for patients, they can be life-saving. A mislabeled drug or improperly stored vaccine can lead to ineffective treatment or severe adverse reactions. In practice, pharmacists often face real-time challenges balancing operational efficiency with meticulous adherence to these requirements.

Another practical compliance concern involves expiry management. Regulatory rules mandate strict tracking and disposal of expired medicines. Pharmacies must remove expired stock from shelves immediately and maintain documentary evidence of safe disposal. Failing to do so invites penalties, but more importantly, poses severe health risks. Pharmacists regularly recount instances where patients unknowingly request products nearing expiry due to familiarity with a particular brand or price-driven preference. Proper workflow design and automated expiry alerts ensure timely stock rotation and safe disposal, preventing accidental harm and demonstrating professional integrity. This meticulous management may seem invisible to customers, but it forms part of the silent infrastructure safeguarding their health.

Waste disposal and environmental compliance represent evolving regulatory areas. The biomedical waste management rules extend responsibilities to pharmacies regarding expired drugs, damaged vials, syringes, and contaminated packaging. While hospitals and large distributors are familiar with medical waste protocols, many smaller pharmacies are still adapting. Training regarding segregation, secure storage of hazardous waste, and authorized disposal mechanisms is increasingly enforced. Regulatory agencies recognize that responsible waste handling contributes to broader public health outcomes, especially in densely populated urban environments where improper disposal could contaminate water or soil. When pharmacies participate actively in environmental compliance, they reinforce the link between good business practices and sustainable public health.

Practical Challenges Retailers Face in Multi-State Operations

The rise of nutraceuticals, herbal supplements, wellness products, and over-the-counter offerings has expanded the scope of retail pharmacy significantly. This growth introduces unique challenges as products governed by the Food Safety and Standards Authority of India differ in regulatory classification from prescription medicines under CDSCO oversight. Pharmacists must educate themselves on dual-compliance expectations, including labeling rules, permissible health claims, and batch certification requirements. While patients may view nutraceuticals as harmless "health boosters," improper usage can lead to interactions with prescription medications or underlying health conditions. This evolving category underscores the pharmacist's role as a knowledge-driven gatekeeper, ensuring customers make informed choices even outside prescription contexts.

In addition to formal compliance, soft-regulation through ethical expectations shapes daily operations. Professional bodies and academic programs emphasize counseling, dosage clarity, and patient privacy as markers of good pharmacy practice. For example, even though privacy laws for pharmacy interactions are less stringent than hospital confidentiality mandates, pharmacists recognize the importance of discrete consultations when discussing sensitive treatments. A patient purchasing antiretroviral therapy, psychiatric drugs, or hormone treatments deserves care beyond the transactional exchange. When pharmacists protect confidentiality, they uphold both ethical trust and the spirit of regulatory frameworks that place patient dignity at the center of healthcare delivery.

Technological adoption continues to reshape compliance readiness. Pharmacies increasingly rely on software that integrates licensing documents, tax compliance, inventory tracking, and storage monitoring into centralized dashboards. These tools assist in audit-readiness, maintain data integrity, and provide automated alerts when compliance risks arise. However, technology alone is insufficient without human oversight and continuous training. The best systems succeed when pharmacists understand their purpose and maintain vigilance over every operation that touches public health. Many operators acknowledge that training and communication have become essential compliance pillars, especially in chains employing large teams with varied educational backgrounds and levels of regulatory familiarity.

Collaboration among industry stakeholders is also critical. Pharmaceutical manufacturers, distributors, e-pharmacy platforms, regulators, and pharmacists together form a compliance ecosystem. Communication gaps between these groups can lead to delays in adverse event reporting, stock shortages of essential medicines, or mishandling of high-risk drugs. Government initiatives encouraging digital prescription formats, shared traceability systems, and harmonized interstate regulations show promise in easing operational burdens while improving oversight. Regular dialogue between private sector leaders and policymakers helps identify practical barriers and guides reforms that support compliance without compromising business sustainability.

The pandemic years created new urgency around regulatory agility. During COVID-19, pharmacies emerged as frontline healthcare touchpoints. Regulatory agencies adapted rapidly, allowing home delivery of certain prescription drugs, fast-tracked licenses, and introduced new protocols for personal protective equipment and sanitization. Pharmacists took on expanded responsibilities, offering triage advice, managing oxygen supply prescriptions, and counseling anxious patients in difficult circumstances. These experiences highlighted the importance of a flexible yet robust regulatory structure—one that can rapidly respond to national health emergencies while maintaining safety and ethical standards. Lessons from the pandemic continue to influence reforms, encouraging digital prescription security, strengthening supply chain surveillance, and revisiting licensing norms for operational scalability during crises.

As India's healthcare infrastructure evolves, pharmacists are increasingly recognized as clinical professionals rather than merely retail operators. Continuous professional development is not formally mandated in all states yet, but policymakers and pharmacy associations widely advocate for its implementation. Mandatory education updates would ensure that pharmacists remain current with regulatory updates, emerging therapies, and evolving patient expectations. Through certification programs and ongoing competency assessments, regulatory agencies can reinforce pharmacy's role as a trusted healthcare conduit. A future in which pharmacists actively engage in preventive care, chronic disease counseling, and therapy adherence monitoring will require greater regulatory clarity and empowered practice rights.

In everyday business, the most successful pharmacies internalize compliance as part of their culture. Leaders set clear expectations that laws and safety standards are non-negotiable, regardless of short-term competitive pressures. Communication across shifts, standardized procedures, and team accountability foster consistency even when operations are complex or fast-paced. When compliance becomes a shared mission rather than an imposed responsibility, pharmacies experience fewer supply disruptions, smoother audits, enhanced patient satisfaction, and stronger brand reputation. In

India's increasingly competitive pharmaceutical retail landscape, integrity can be a powerful differentiator.

Some of the challenges faced today will evolve with time, but the core purpose of pharmacy regulations will remain unchanged: to ensure that every medicine dispensed contributes to healing rather than harm. Regulatory frameworks act as a guiding backbone that prevents shortcuts which could risk patient lives. In a sector dependent on precision, trust, and scientific rigor, even small lapses can lead to significant consequences. This accountability underscores why regulatory compliance should not be perceived as an administrative burden. It is a commitment to public welfare, an affirmation of the pharmacist's professional identity, and a daily reaffirmation that patient safety comes first.

Moving forward, regulatory modernization will likely continue in step with technological progress. Artificial intelligence may support drug interaction alerts at the point of sale. Blockchain systems may secure supply chain transparency, ensuring that every product can be authenticated from factory to consumer. Cloud-based compliance records may eliminate paperwork inefficiencies and enhance cross-border synchronization for multi-state operations. Each advancement further strengthens patient safeguards while reducing operational obstacles for pharmacists. However, adopting innovation requires careful balancing of cost, practicality, and staff adaptability. Regulatory policies must support transition without excluding small or independent pharmacies that form the backbone of healthcare in many parts of India.

The trust between pharmacies and regulators is built on openness and mutual understanding. Regulators aim to protect public health, not hinder legitimate business growth. Pharmacies that maintain transparency during audits, report discrepancies proactively, and embrace corrective measures often establish cooperative rather than adversarial relationships with authorities. This collaborative approach improves outcomes for both sides, reduces enforcement tension, and supports the broader national goal of accessible, safe, and efficient healthcare delivery.

Ultimately, compliance in pharmaceutical retail is a journey rather than a destination. Laws evolve, expectations shift, scientific knowledge grows, and the healthcare landscape transforms with each passing year. Pharmacies that thrive over decades are those that adapt continuously, invest in learning, and align their purpose with public well-being. Through every prescription dispensed, every counseling session conducted, and every regulatory requirement met, pharmacies contribute to a healthier India. Compliance, therefore, is not only about fulfilling legal duties. It is about honoring the trust placed in pharmacists by every individual who steps into the pharmacy seeking relief, reassurance, and care.

Pharmacy regulations in India form a sophisticated yet practical shield that protects millions of lives every day. From the smallest neighborhood counter to the largest online platform, compliance ensures that medications remain instruments of healing. When pharmacies embrace this framework fully, they elevate both their professional value and their role as essential community health partners. The result is a healthcare system grounded in trust, driven by ethics, and capable of supporting the nation's wellness aspirations long into the future.

In conclusion, the regulatory and compliance landscape in Indian pharmacy retail is both extensive and essential. Licensing, taxation, drug schedules, storage, labeling, digital integration, multi-state operations, inspections, and ongoing professional development form the core pillars of compliance. These measures are not bureaucratic hurdles but deliberate safeguards designed to protect patients, uphold professional integrity, and maintain public confidence. For pharmacy operators, understanding and embedding these frameworks into daily operations ensures operational resilience, legal adherence, and a high standard of patient care. Compliance, in this sense, is not just a legal requirement; it is the foundation upon which the pharmacy's reputation, effectiveness, and societal value are built. In a sector that bridges commerce and care, the regulatory framework provides clarity, guidance, and a pathway to responsible, ethical, and sustainable pharmacy practice.

References

- Drugs and Cosmetics Act, 1940. Ministry of Health and Family Welfare. https://cdsco.gov.in/opencms/opencms/en/Acts-Rules/
- Drugs and Cosmetics Rules, 1945. Ministry of Health and Family Welfare. https://cdsco.gov.in/opencms/opencms/en/Acts-Rules/
- Central Drugs Standard Control Organization (CDSCO) Official Website. https://cdsco.gov.in/
- Food Safety and Standards Authority of India (FSSAI) Official Website. https://fssai.gov.in/
- Schedule H, H1, and X drug guidelines. Ministry of Health and Family Welfare.https://dcaodisha.nic.in/sites/default/files/Schedule%20H1%20Drugs.pdf
- GST Council: Impact on Pharmaceuticals. https://www.gst.gov.in/
- Pradhan Mantri Bhartiya Janaushadhi Pariyojana Guidelines. Government of India. https://janaushadhi.gov.in/?utm_source
- Indian Journal of Pharmacy Practice. https://www.ijopp.org/
- Indian Journal of Pharmaceutical Education and Research. https://www.ijper.org/
- CDSCO Annual Report 2023. https://cdsco.gov.in/

- Multi-State Pharmacy Operations and Compliance Challenges, Indian Journal of Pharmacy Operationsz https://ijme.in/wp-content/uploads/2025/05/COMMENTARY-Haripriya-1.pdf
- Draft E-Pharmacy Rules (2018)—IndusLaw PDF
- https://induslaw.com/publications/pdf/alerts-2018/Draft_E_pharmacy_Rules.pdf INDUSLAW
- "Regulation of E-Pharmacies in India" – IBA (International Bar Association)
- https://www.ibanet.org/e-pharmacies-and-the-law-an-uneasy-balance IBA
- "The rise of E-pharmacy in India: Benefits, challenges, and the road ahead"—PMC article
- https://www.ncbi.nlm.nih.gov/pmc/articles/PMC9804119/

Chapter 3

Role of Key Stakeholders

Pharmaceutical retail is not a single enterprise but a complex ecosystem woven together by people, institutions, and regulations. Behind every prescription filled or medicine dispensed lies a coordinated effort involving multiple layers of stakeholders, manufacturers, distributors, pharmacists, regulators, and healthcare professionals. Each plays a distinct role, yet none operates in isolation. The success of pharmacy retail depends on how effectively these entities collaborate, balance commercial objectives with ethical responsibilities, and adapt to the ever-changing healthcare environment.

In understanding this network, it becomes clear that the strength of the pharmaceutical retail system lies not merely in its infrastructure or technology but in its relationships. These connections, from supplier to retailer, from pharmacist to patient, form the backbone of a system that directly influences public health outcomes. To grasp the true nature of pharma retail, one must first understand the people and organisations that make it function.

The Backbone of Distribution: Wholesalers, Distributors, and C&F Agents

The journey of a medicine from factory to pharmacy counter may seem straightforward to the casual observer, but in reality, it is a meticulously managed logistical operation. Once a pharmaceutical company manufactures its products, the responsibility for ensuring they reach retailers across the country lies with wholesalers, distributors, and clearing and forwarding (C&F) agents.

Wholesalers act as the first bridge between pharmaceutical companies and retailers. Their primary role is to purchase large quantities of medicines from manufacturers or super-stockists and redistribute them in smaller lots to retail pharmacies. This system ensures that pharmacies in every city, town, and rural area have access to a consistent supply of medicines without needing to engage directly with manufacturers. Wholesalers also play a crucial role in balancing inventory levels, managing product rotation, and ensuring that life-saving drugs are available even in remote areas where demand may fluctuate unpredictably.

C&F agents, on the other hand, are the logistical nerve centres of the pharmaceutical supply chain. Appointed by manufacturers, they handle warehousing, order processing, and transportation. In India, where the pharmaceutical distribution system operates on a multi-tier model, C&F agents manage regional hubs that feed distributors and wholesalers within their zones. They are responsible for maintaining cold chain conditions, adhering to storage standards, and ensuring that regulatory documentation is complete before medicines move further downstream.

Distributors serve as intermediaries who deal directly with retail pharmacies. They often carry multiple product lines from various manufacturers, helping retailers source diverse brands conveniently. The distributor's role goes beyond simple delivery; they handle credit management, ensure timely replenishment, and serve as information channels about new product launches, shortages, and policy changes. In an industry governed by expiry dates and compliance regulations, distributors are also accountable for product traceability, batch verification, and managing returns for expired or damaged goods.

This intricate structure has evolved over decades, balancing efficiency with control. The Central Drugs Standard Control Organisation (CDSCO) and state-level authorities enforce regulations that govern the licensing and operations of these intermediaries. Without their diligence, the pharmaceutical retail sector would struggle to maintain both accessibility and safety standards.

However, the distribution network is not without challenges. India's vast geography, diverse climates, and fragmented logistics infrastructure can complicate timely delivery. Temperature-sensitive medicines require strict cold chain management, which demands investment in insulated vehicles and temperature-controlled warehouses. The Goods and Services Tax (GST) regime brought standardisation in taxation, but it also required distributors and wholesalers to overhaul their invoicing and compliance systems. Despite these hurdles, the distribution network remains the lifeline of India's healthcare retail sector, ensuring that essential medicines reach every corner of the country.

The Pharmacist: The Human Face of Pharmacy Retail

Among all stakeholders, the pharmacist occupies a uniquely personal role. For most patients, the pharmacist is the first, and often the most frequent, point of contact within the healthcare system. While doctors diagnose and prescribe, it is the pharmacist who translates those prescriptions into tangible care. Beyond dispensing medicines, they explain dosage schedules, potential side effects, and drug interactions. In doing so, they bridge the gap between clinical advice and patient understanding.

Ethical selling is at the core of the pharmacist's profession. Every day, pharmacists balance commercial imperatives with moral responsibility. They are custodians of drugs that can heal but also harm if misused. In India, regulations such as Schedule H, H1, and X of the Drugs and Cosmetics Act strictly govern which medicines can be sold only on prescription. Yet, compliance relies heavily on the pharmacist's integrity. Selling antibiotics, sedatives, or narcotics without valid prescriptions can have serious public health implications, from drug abuse to antimicrobial resistance. The best pharmacists recognise their pivotal role in curbing these risks through vigilance and education.

The modern pharmacist's role has evolved significantly in recent years. Pharmacies are no longer mere points of sale; they are emerging as community health hubs. Pharmacists now offer services such as blood pressure monitoring, vaccination assistance, and medication counselling. The introduction of patient data management tools allows them to track adherence patterns and provide reminders for chronic disease medications. As India grapples with rising lifestyle disorders like diabetes and hypertension, the pharmacist's role in promoting adherence and preventive care has become indispensable.

Yet, the profession also faces its set of challenges. Many retail pharmacists in India operate under tight margins, constrained by competitive pricing and limited bargaining power against distributors. Staffing shortages, inadequate continuing education opportunities, and limited digital integration can affect both service quality and compliance. Nonetheless, where pharmacists rise above these limitations, they become trusted allies in community health, embodying the human touch that technology alone cannot replicate.

Partnerships with Healthcare Professionals

The relationship between pharmacists and healthcare professionals forms the foundation of effective patient care. Traditionally, this partnership was limited, doctors prescribed, and pharmacists dispensed. However, as healthcare systems evolved, the need for greater collaboration became apparent. Today, pharmacists and doctors increasingly work together to ensure safe, rational, and effective use of medicines.

In hospital settings, clinical pharmacists collaborate directly with physicians during ward rounds, advising on drug selection, dosage adjustments, and monitoring for side effects. In retail settings, the collaboration is more informal yet equally crucial. Pharmacists often clarify ambiguous prescriptions, suggest generic alternatives, or alert doctors to potential drug interactions reported by patients. These interactions enhance patient safety and optimise treatment outcomes.

The integration of digital prescription systems has further improved coordination between pharmacists and healthcare professionals. Electronic Medical Records (EMR) and e-prescriptions reduce errors caused by illegible handwriting or dosage confusion. Some urban pharmacy chains in India have started offering teleconsultation services, connecting patients directly with qualified doctors through their digital platforms. In this setup, pharmacists act as facilitators, helping patients transition smoothly from consultation to medication.

Collaborative partnerships also extend to public health initiatives. During vaccination drives or health awareness campaigns, pharmacists often assist doctors and nurses by handling logistics, patient registration, and counselling. During the COVID-19 pandemic, for instance, pharmacists played an instrumental role in managing medicine supply chains, distributing protective equipment, and guiding communities about preventive measures. Their proximity to the community made them invaluable allies in healthcare delivery at the grassroots level.

Government Bodies and Regulatory Oversight

In India, oversight begins with the Central Drugs Standard Control Organisation (CDSCO) and extends through state-level drug control departments. Together, they form the legal and administrative framework that ensures medicines are safe, effective, and properly distributed.

The CDSCO functions under the Ministry of Health and Family Welfare, serving as India's national regulatory authority. It is responsible for approving new drugs, conducting clinical trial oversight, and ensuring compliance with the Drugs and Cosmetics Act of 1940. State regulators, on the other hand, handle licensing and inspections for manufacturing, distribution, and retail operations within their jurisdictions. This dual system helps maintain both national uniformity and regional accountability.

Government agencies also play a vital role in price regulation. The National Pharmaceutical Pricing Authority (NPPA) monitors and enforces price ceilings under the Drugs (Prices Control) Order, ensuring essential medicines remain affordable. Meanwhile, the Food Safety and Standards Authority of India (FSSAI) oversees the sale of nutraceuticals, supplements, and other health-related products that share shelf space with pharmaceuticals.

Policymaking in this sector is not static. Over the years, reforms such as the introduction of GST, e-pharmacy guidelines, and digital health frameworks have reshaped operations at every level. These initiatives aim to bring transparency, improve traceability, and curb counterfeit drug circulation. The implementation of barcode systems for medicine packaging and e-license portals are examples of regulatory innovation that make compliance easier while protecting public health.

However, regulation is also a double-edged sword. While it ensures safety and fairness, it can sometimes create operational hurdles, especially for small retailers. Licensing procedures, documentation requirements, and state-level variations in interpretation can slow down business processes. The key lies in dialogue, an ongoing conversation between regulators and industry stakeholders that balances enforcement with practicality.

Interdependencies Across the Supply Chain

If one were to visualise pharmaceutical retail as a network, it would resemble an intricate web of interdependencies. Manufacturers depend on wholesalers and distributors to extend their market reach. Retailers rely on distributors for timely supplies and credit flexibility. Regulators depend on all parties for accurate reporting, while patients depend on everyone in the chain for safety and reliability.

Manufacturers initiate the process by producing formulations that meet therapeutic needs and regulatory standards. They provide batch details, quality certifications, and marketing materials that flow downstream. Distributors handle the logistics and financial transactions, while retailers close the loop by delivering the product to the end user. Breakdowns at any point, be it supply disruption, non-compliance, or misinformation, can have a domino effect across the chain.

Collaboration is therefore not optional; it is fundamental. Many companies have begun adopting integrated supply chain management systems that allow real-time visibility across stakeholders. For instance, Enterprise Resource Planning (ERP) tools enable tracking of stock movements, expiry dates, and credit cycles. Such systems not only improve efficiency but also strengthen trust among partners.

Financial interdependence is another defining feature. Pharmacies often operate on credit extended by distributors, who in turn rely on timely payments from retailers to maintain liquidity. This delicate balance is managed through personal relationships, reputation, and adherence to agreed credit terms. Inconsistent payments or delayed settlements can strain the entire network, highlighting how financial discipline is as critical as regulatory compliance in maintaining system stability.

If the pharmaceutical retail ecosystem were to be drawn out on paper, it would not resemble a neat flowchart but a living network, a web where every thread is connected, and the pull at one end can instantly ripple across to the other. This interconnection is what sustains the system and, at times, what makes it vulnerable. In the world of medicine, where a single delayed delivery or compliance lapse can affect patient outcomes, interdependence is not merely a structural characteristic; it is the foundation of trust that holds the entire supply chain together.

At the very beginning of this web stand the manufacturers. They are the creators, formulating drugs that meet both therapeutic needs and the stringent expectations of regulatory authorities. Their role doesn't end once the medicine leaves the factory floor. Each batch that moves out carries with it a story of quality checks, of compliance certifications, of the careful balancing act between cost, efficacy, and accessibility. These batches are then handed over to distributors and clearing & forwarding agents (C&F) who are tasked with translating production into reach.

Distributors are the arteries of the system. They take the product from a manufacturer's warehouse and ensure it reaches every pharmacy, hospital, and institution that needs it. This stage demands efficiency, accuracy, and an almost obsessive commitment to timelines. A delay of even a day can lead to a shortage that ripples all the way down to the patient. The relationship between manufacturer and distributor is therefore not transactional; it is symbiotic. Both depend on each other for continuity. A manufacturer without reliable distributors is like a car without wheels, and a distributor without trusted manufacturers has nothing to move.

Then come the retailers, who sit at the heart of the supply chain's final mile. They are the face of the pharmaceutical industry to the public. Every pill that changes hands at a pharmacy counter is the end result of thousands of coordinated actions across this web.

Retailers depend on distributors for timely stock replenishment, but they also rely on them for flexibility, extended credit periods, stock returns, and support during regulatory inspections.

The regulatory bodies, whether central or state-level, act as the balancing force ensuring that all participants adhere to the same moral and procedural compass. Their role is not limited to inspection or penalty. They shape the framework that defines how these relationships operate, through rules that determine everything from labeling and storage conditions to prescription requirements and audit trails. In turn, regulators depend on each stakeholder for transparency and accurate reporting. If a retailer fails to maintain sales records or a distributor does not update batch numbers in real time, the regulatory chain weakens.

At the far end of this network lies the patient, the most critical link of all. They depend on everyone, on the manufacturer for drug quality, on the distributor for supply consistency, on the retailer for authenticity, and on regulators for safety oversight. In that sense, the patient is not outside the chain but an invisible force that binds it together.

A production delay at the manufacturing end can trigger cascading shortages across regions. A documentation lapse at the distributor's warehouse can halt shipments. A pricing dispute between retailer and distributor can affect access to essential medicines in entire localities. These are not hypothetical scenarios; they play out often and serve as reminders that the system's success depends not on individual performance, but on collective discipline and cooperation.

For years, pharmaceutical businesses operated in silos. Each player guarded their data and processes closely, believing control was key to stability. But the modern retail ecosystem has shown that transparency, not secrecy, builds resilience. Today, leading companies are adopting integrated supply chain management systems that offer real-time visibility across all levels, from manufacturing lines to pharmacy counters.

Enterprise Resource Planning (ERP) tools, for example, have transformed how information travels. A pharmacist in Jaipur can now check stock levels of a product in a distributor's warehouse in Ahmedabad and place an order that syncs automatically with the manufacturer's production plan. Expiry dates, batch numbers, and even credit limits can be monitored within a single digital environment. This interconnectedness doesn't just improve operational efficiency, it builds confidence among partners.

Beyond logistics and technology lies the invisible yet powerful network of financial interdependence. Pharmacies often run on credit extended by distributors, which can range from a few days to several weeks. This informal arrangement, deeply rooted in mutual trust, is the lifeblood of retail operations in India. A distributor's willingness to extend credit to a retailer is often based not on formal documentation but on the reputation that retailer has built over years.

This trust-based credit ecosystem is both beautiful and fragile. It allows small independent chemists to survive in competitive markets, but it also requires immense discipline. When payments are delayed, distributors struggle to maintain their own liquidity, affecting their ability to purchase from manufacturers. The entire system then begins to strain under financial pressure.

Many established distributors handle this by creating layered credit systems, granting shorter credit cycles to newer retailers while allowing longer ones to those with proven track records. Similarly, retailers who consistently clear dues on time often receive priority during stock shortages. These unwritten rules sustain the delicate financial equilibrium of the industry.

The relationship between trust and compliance is also noteworthy. When partners honour their commitments, whether financial, operational, or regulatory, the system thrives. But when shortcuts are taken, the effects are immediate. A single counterfeit batch or delayed payment can disrupt long-standing business ties. In this sense, compliance is not just about satisfying a rulebook; it is about preserving credibility in a chain built on interdependence.

Interdependence is not only about physical goods and money. It is also about information. The pharmaceutical retail system runs on data, about prescriptions, demand patterns, product recalls, and new launches. The timeliness and accuracy of this information determine how effectively the network functions.

While technology and systems have become central, the pharmaceutical retail chain still runs on human relationships. Most distributors know their retailers personally. Many have decades-long associations that extend beyond business. Similarly, pharmacists often have a personal rapport with company representatives who visit their stores. These human bonds form a layer of resilience that no algorithm can replace.

Looking ahead, the concept of interdependence is likely to deepen rather than diminish. The rise of digital pharmacies, the integration of AI-driven inventory systems, and the government's focus on National Digital Health Mission (NDHM) are all pushing stakeholders toward even tighter collaboration. Manufacturers are exploring blockchain-based traceability to ensure product authenticity, while distributors are automating warehouses to improve turnaround times. Retailers, on their part, are adopting point-of-sale systems that integrate directly with supply chain software.

However, technology alone will not define the next phase. The strength of the system will continue to depend on trust, transparency, and ethical collaboration, values that have always defined the best of India's pharmaceutical community.

The pharmaceutical retail supply chain is, at its core, a reflection of human intention. It is about people working together under shared responsibility to deliver something that matters more than profit: health. The links that connect manufacturers, distributors, retailers, regulators, and patients are not just commercial transactions; they are commitments of trust repeated every single day. And that, perhaps, is the real story of interdependence in this remarkable ecosystem.

Real-World Examples of Collaboration

Several examples illustrate how cooperation among stakeholders can drive both business success and public health benefits. During the COVID-19 crisis, pharmaceutical distributors and retailers worked round the clock to maintain the supply of critical medicines, oxygen supplies, and sanitizers. Collaboration between the government, manufacturers, and logistics providers ensured that essential drugs reached even the most affected regions despite lockdown restrictions.

In India, initiatives such as the Pradhan Mantri Bhartiya Janaushadhi Pariyojana (PMBJP) demonstrate effective collaboration between public and private sectors. Manufacturers supply generic medicines at controlled prices, distributors handle logistics, and licensed retailers operate dedicated Janaushadhi outlets that provide affordable access to essential drugs. This model showcases how coordinated effort across stakeholders can achieve both economic and social impact.

Globally, partnerships have taken similar forms. In the UK, collaborations between the National Health Service (NHS) and community pharmacies have expanded access to vaccinations and chronic disease monitoring. In the United States, chain pharmacies have integrated digital prescriptions with insurance systems, creating seamless coordination between patients, providers, and payers. These examples underline that stakeholder collaboration, when structured and transparent, benefits everyone in the ecosystem.

The pharmaceutical retail industry is a collective enterprise built on trust, expertise, and shared responsibility. Each stakeholder, from the manufacturer formulating a new drug to the pharmacist dispensing it, contributes to a larger mission of improving human health. The system thrives not merely on transactions but on relationships grounded in accountability and cooperation.

As the industry evolves, collaboration among stakeholders will continue to define its progress. The introduction of technology, regulatory reforms, and changing patient expectations are reshaping traditional boundaries. Yet, the essence remains constant: ensuring that safe, effective, and affordable medicines reach every individual who needs them.

The story of pharma retail, therefore, is not just about commerce; it is about coordination. It is a testament to what happens when diverse entities align around a common purpose: the preservation and improvement of life itself.

References

- Central Drugs Standard Control Organisation (CDSCO) – https://cdsco.gov.in
- National Pharmaceutical Pricing Authority (NPPA) – https://www.nppaindia.nic.in
- Food Safety and Standards Authority of India (FSSAI) – https://www.fssai.gov.in
- Department of Pharmaceuticals, Government of India – https://pharmaceuticals.gov.in
- World Health Organization: "Role of Pharmacists in Health Systems" https://www.who.int
- "India's Pharma Supply Chain : Does the Industry Have What It Takes to Win?" Organisation of Pharmaceutical Producers of India & Indian Pharmaceutical Association report (2019)—https://www.indiaoppi.com/wp-content/

uploads/2019/12/Indias-Pharma-Supply-Chain-Does-the-Industry-Have-What-It-Takes-to-Win.pdf

- "Changing Dynamics of Indian Pharma Supply Chain" Indian Pharmaceutical Association (IPA) report (2024)—https://www.ipa-india.org/sites/default/files/2025-07/ChangingDynamics-of-Indian-PharmaSupplychain-1.pdf
- "Indian Pharmaceutical Industry's Supply Chain Challenges" (PNR Journal)—https://www.pnrjournal.com/index.php/home/article/download/5356/6430/6582
- Study of Logistics Issues in the Indian Pharmaceutical Industry"—Puri S., Ranjan J., Int. J. Logistics Economics & Globalisation, Vol 4, No 3, 2012 https://www.researchgate.net/publication/264821685_Study_of_logistics_issues_in_the_Indian_pharmaceutical_industry
- India Flags Testing Lapses at Pharma Firms after Cough Syrup Deaths"—Reuters, 8 October 2025. https://www.reuters.com/business/healthcare-pharmaceuticals/india-flags-testing-lapses-pharma-firms-after-cough-syrups-deaths-2025-10-08

Chapter 4

Business Models in Pharma Retail

Every pharmacy, no matter how small or large, begins with the same foundation, a promise of trust. People walk into a chemist shop not merely to buy a product but to find relief, reassurance, and reliability. Behind the counter, however, lies a far more intricate story than just prescriptions and shelves of medicines. There is an entire business design at work, one that shapes how efficiently the pharmacy runs, how profitable it can be, and how well it sustains that trust over time.

The business of pharmacy retail in India has evolved dramatically in the past two decades. What began as a largely unorganised trade dominated by standalone chemists has now transformed into a layered and competitive marketplace. Today's pharmacy sector includes everything from neighbourhood stores run by families to vast, data-driven retail networks managed by corporate giants. In this transformation, business models have become the real differentiator. The model you choose defines everything, from your investment appetite and operational control to your scalability and long-term survival.

In India, where healthcare access is uneven and regulatory frameworks are complex, choosing the right model is both an art and a science. Some operators prioritise tight control over operations and brand uniformity. Others focus on speed and scale through partnerships. Many now attempt a blend, marrying corporate discipline with local entrepreneurship. As we go deeper into this chapter, we will explore the three dominant business models that power India's pharma retail industry—company-owned, franchise, and hybrid systems.

We will also unpack the economics behind these structures, evaluate ROI and breakeven benchmarks, and study the journeys of Apollo Pharmacy, MedPlus, and key regional players. Finally, we will examine what makes a model scalable and sustainable in India's complex regulatory and cultural landscape.

Company-Owned, Franchise, and Hybrid Models

The choice between owning, franchising, or blending both models is not a simple financial decision. It is a statement about how much control a business wants to retain and how much trust it places in partners to represent its brand.

A company-owned model is the most direct way of building a pharmacy network. Here, the parent organisation owns or leases each store, hires employees, manages operations, and controls every process from inventory procurement to customer experience. This model works best when a brand's primary goal is consistency and control. The stores look the same, follow identical SOPs, use the same digital systems, and deliver uniform service. Customers know what to expect whether they visit a branch in Chennai or Chandigarh. This predictability builds brand credibility.

However, this model comes with a heavy cost. Owning every store means committing large capital upfront, not just for infrastructure but also for working capital, inventory, and staff. Managing hundreds of stores requires a centralised supply chain, regional operations teams, and a deep investment in training and technology. Only companies with strong financial backing and operational maturity can sustain this. Yet, the payoff is real. Central control allows such chains to experiment with new ideas—wellness programs, digital ordering, or pharmacy-linked diagnostics—and roll them out quickly across their network.

The franchise model offers a different rhythm. Instead of building every store itself, a brand licenses its systems, name, and business processes to independent entrepreneurs who open and run stores under its banner. The franchisee invests the capital, manages day-to-day operations, and earns profits after paying fees or a share of revenue to the franchisor. For the franchisor, this approach enables rapid expansion with minimal capital burden. For the franchisee, it reduces risk because they are entering a proven business framework rather than starting from zero.

Franchising has fuelled much of the organised pharmacy expansion in India's smaller towns and semi-urban clusters. It brings in local ownership, which often translates to better customer relationships and regional understanding. Yet, it also creates a challenge: maintaining uniformity across outlets owned by different people. To manage this, successful pharmacy franchisors invest heavily in audits, supply chain integration, and digital monitoring. They ensure that pricing, storage, and documentation standards meet compliance norms regardless of location.

Between these two models lies the hybrid approach, a structure that blends corporate control with entrepreneurial participation. In a hybrid model, a company might operate flagship outlets in metros while franchising or partnering in smaller cities. Some hybrids use a revenue-sharing system where the brand manages procurement and branding while local entrepreneurs handle sales. Others build joint ventures with local investors. The logic is simple: retain strategic control where brand visibility matters, and delegate where local expertise adds value.

The hybrid model is increasingly popular among mid-sized pharmacy chains. It allows them to manage risk and growth simultaneously. They can test innovations in company-owned stores, learn what works, and then scale through franchise or partnership formats. It is also a flexible model that adapts well to India's diversity, where every region has different consumer habits, doctor networks, and pricing expectations.

Each of these structures, company-owned, franchise, and hybrid, is valid. The right choice depends on the founder's financial bandwidth, appetite for control, and long-term vision. A corporate may prefer ownership to maintain brand precision. An investor seeking faster ROI may lean toward franchising. A regional player expanding into new territories may find hybrid the perfect balance. What truly matters is clarity of intent and discipline of execution.

ROI and Breakeven Benchmarks

Pharmacy retail is a steady business. Unlike fashion or electronics, medicines do not go out of trend. People fall sick, recover, and return, a predictable cycle that keeps cash registers ticking. But predictability alone does not guarantee profitability. The economics of pharmacy retail are tight, and every operator, whether corporate or independent, must understand what drives ROI and when breakeven can realistically occur.

Setting up a pharmacy requires both one-time and recurring investments. Initial costs include premises rent or lease deposits, furniture and fixtures, refrigeration units, point-of-sale systems, computers, licenses, and initial inventory. In metros, setup costs are significantly higher due to rent, while in tier-two or tier-three cities, costs may drop by 20–30%. Yet, inventory remains the biggest financial commitment. A store must maintain a broad range of medicines, including fast-moving generics and slower-moving specialities, to meet prescription diversity.

Margins vary sharply across product types. Prescription drugs (especially branded ones) often yield low gross margins of 10–15%, while OTC items and wellness products can provide 25–40%. Generics offer high percentage margins but smaller volumes. A smart retailer, therefore, balances all three categories, branded drugs for consistency, OTC for profitability, and generics for competitive pricing. The result is a portfolio that keeps both the accountant and the customer happy.

On average, a standalone pharmacy can expect to reach breakeven within 9 to 18 months, depending on rent, competition, and sales velocity. Franchised outlets sometimes hit breakeven faster (in 6–12 months) because they receive training, supplier discounts, and brand-driven marketing support. Company-owned outlets, with their heavier overheads, might take longer but benefit from stronger long-term margins and resale value.

Operational discipline is the real differentiator. A store that tracks stock turnover, negotiates better credit terms, and uses software to avoid expiry losses can achieve healthy returns even in crowded markets. Conversely, lack of oversight can eat margins fast. Overstaffing, delayed supplier payments, or excessive discounting can erode profitability in months.

From an investor's perspective, ROI in pharmacy retail is steady rather than spectacular. Annual returns of 15–25% are common for well-managed outlets, higher if the business expands into wellness or diagnostics. For franchisors and corporates, the aggregate ROI improves through scale, bulk procurement, shared logistics, and centralised marketing. For small entrepreneurs, pharmacy remains one of the few retail categories that offer consistent earnings and goodwill.

The financial equation is simple but unforgiving: control inventory, control cash flow, and control compliance. Those who get these three right rarely fail.

Case Examples of Apollo, MedPlus, and Regional Chains

Studying real-world cases is the best way to understand how business models behave outside theory. In India, the two most studied pharmacy chains are Apollo Pharmacy and MedPlus, each following a different route to scale. Around them exist dozens of strong regional networks that thrive quietly in their territories. Together, they tell the story of India's evolving pharmacy ecosystem.

Apollo Pharmacy began as an extension of the Apollo Hospitals group. Its early advantage was trust, a reputation built through years of clinical credibility. Apollo used this foundation to create a pharmacy network that assured customers of genuine medicines and professional service. Over the years, Apollo adopted a largely company-owned structure for its core stores while experimenting with partner and franchise outlets in newer markets. This hybridised corporate model allowed Apollo to maintain tight control in strategic zones while expanding its footprint in semi-urban areas.

Its success lies in integration. Apollo has always viewed pharmacy as a gateway to holistic healthcare, linking prescriptions to diagnostics, wellness services, and digital ordering. The company's focus on technology, CRM, and standardised processes made it one of India's largest organised pharmacy chains. According to Apollo HealthCo's public filings, it continues to expand through both physical outlets and digital channels, leveraging brand trust as its competitive moat.

MedPlus, by contrast, was born without a hospital legacy. Founded in Hyderabad, it began as a regional chain and expanded methodically across states. MedPlus's strength lies in operational efficiency and data discipline. It built strong supply chain infrastructure and an omnichannel model long before "omnichannel" became a buzzword. Today, it operates thousands of stores while maintaining profitability—proof that scale and discipline can coexist.

MedPlus followed a mix of company-owned and franchise formats depending on market maturity. It invested early in back-end logistics, ensuring that stores rarely faced stockouts. Its loyalty programs and home delivery integrations created a steady customer base. When MedPlus went public, analysts noted its ability to combine strong same-store growth with prudent expansion, a balance few retail networks achieve.

While Apollo and MedPlus dominate headlines, regional pharmacy chains continue to shape local markets in powerful ways. In southern states like Tamil Nadu and Kerala, chains such as Trust Chemists and MedPlus Local Partners hold loyal clientele. In Maharashtra and Gujarat, groups like Wellness Forever built on local goodwill and proximity service. These regional players thrive because they understand local doctors, festivals, and patient needs. They often achieve faster breakeven by operating lean and avoiding heavy marketing spends. Their success reminds us that pharmacy retail in India is not a winner-takes-all game; it is a mosaic of many strong, regionally rooted players.

Comparing these examples reveals a crucial insight: the model matters less than the discipline behind it. Apollo's corporate control, MedPlus's data-driven hybrid, and the regional players' community roots all succeed for the same reason—they know their customers, manage their inventory well, and comply meticulously with regulations. That is the heart of sustainable pharmacy retail.

Evaluating Scalability and Operational Control

Scaling a pharmacy network is not merely about adding more stores. True scalability means replicating quality, compliance, and customer experience without dilution. The tension between growth and control defines how successful a model can become.

Company-owned models offer direct control. The brand decides everything—store layout, inventory standards, training, and pricing. It can introduce digital innovations, implement automated inventory management, and roll out new services uniformly. This control ensures consistency but limits speed. Every new store requires capital, management bandwidth, and compliance oversight.

Franchise models, in contrast, prioritise speed over central control. By empowering local entrepreneurs, they can open dozens of outlets quickly. But the risk lies in uneven execution. Some franchisees might maintain high standards, while others may compromise on service or documentation. To counter this, successful franchisors use technology, POS integrations, automated reporting, temperature monitoring, and surprise audits to ensure adherence. They also create incentive programs that reward compliant and high-performing franchisees, turning them into long-term partners rather than short-term investors.

Hybrid systems sit in the middle. They grant autonomy but reserve control over the essentials: brand guidelines, procurement channels, and compliance. Many modern pharmacy networks adopt this structure because it scales well while safeguarding brand integrity. It also encourages innovation at the local level. A hybrid network can test a digital health kiosk in a metro flagship store and later roll it out through franchisees if it works.

Scalability also depends on supply chain maturity. The larger the network, the more complex the logistics. Chains with centralised warehouses and regional distribution hubs enjoy economies of scale. They can negotiate better prices, ensure faster replenishment, and maintain temperature-controlled logistics for sensitive drugs. Smaller or loosely structured networks struggle with stock consistency and expiry losses.

Equally critical is people management. Every successful chain invests heavily in training pharmacists and store staff. Knowledge gaps in dosage, documentation, or compliance can lead to penalties and loss of trust. Large chains like Apollo and MedPlus have internal academies to train new recruits. Regional players often partner with local pharmacy colleges. Building a learning culture is the only way to scale without eroding service quality.

Finally, scalability in India is deeply influenced by regulatory complexity. Each state has its own licensing processes and documentation requirements. For a network to grow nationally, it must invest in legal compliance systems, temperature tracking, audit trails, and digital recordkeeping. Many organised players now employ compliance officers or use software that alerts stores when licenses or permits are nearing expiry.

Operational control, therefore, is not about micromanagement. It is about creating systems that self-correct. When a network can monitor, train, and replenish itself with minimal intervention, it becomes truly scalable.

The evolution of India's pharmacy retail sector is as much a story of business models as it is of medicines. From company-owned giants to ambitious franchise chains and flexible hybrids, every format reflects a different philosophy of growth. Some prioritise uniformity, others agility, and many now aim for balance.

What remains common is the foundation: trust, discipline, and compliance. Pharmacies exist at the intersection of healthcare and commerce. Every pill sold carries both a profit margin and a moral obligation. The best business models are those that respect both.

The future will likely belong to adaptable hybrids—systems that use data and digital tools to maintain control while empowering local entrepreneurs. As healthcare becomes more technology-driven, these networks will expand into diagnostics, preventive care, and e-pharmacy services. But their heart will remain the same: a promise to deliver the right medicine at the right time, with honesty and care.

References

- "India Retail Pharmacy Market Size, Share and Forecast 2032"—Credence Research. https://www.credenceresearch.com/report/india-retail-pharmacy-market

- "India Retail Pharmacy Market Size, Growth, Share and Forecast 2032"—Credence Research. https://www.credenceresearch.com/report/retail-pharmacy-market
- "India Pharmacy Market Size & Outlook, 2024-2030"—Grand View Research. https://www.grandviewresearch.com/horizon/outlook/pharmacy-market/india
- "Apollo Pharmacies Limited – Rating Rationale"—CRISIL Ratings (May 2024). https://www.crisilratings.com/mnt/winshare/Ratings/RatingList/RatingDocs/ApolloPharmaciesLimited_May%2023_%202024_RR_339062.html
- "Apollo Pharmacies Limited – Rating Rationale"—CRISIL Ratings (May 2025). https://www.crisilratings.com/mnt/winshare/Ratings/RatingList/RatingDocs/ApolloPharmaciesLimited_May%2020_%202025_RR_366543.html
- "India Online and Offline Pharmacy Retail Market Outlook to 2025"—Ken Research. https://www.kenresearch.com/industry-reports/india-online-offline-pharmacy-retail-market
- ScienceDirect. "Supply Chain and Online Pharmacy Logistics in India." https://www.sciencedirect.com/science/article/pii/S266618882500855X
- FranchiseIndia. "Top 10 Pharmacy Franchises in India: Cost, Benefits & Requirements." FranchiseIndia Insights. https://www.franchiseindia.com/insights/en/article/top-10-pharmacy-franchises-in-india-cost-benefits-and-requirements.57400
- Indian Journal of Pharmaceutical Education and Research (IJPER). "Multi-State Pharmacy Operations and Compliance Challenges." IJPER, 2021. https://www.ijper.org/

Chapter 5

Location, Store Design & Inventory Planning

When you first imagine opening a pharmacy, you might picture jars of pills, a friendly pharmacist, and the gentle chime of a bell as customers walk in. But behind that friendly façade lies a deeply strategic question: Where should the store be? And once you fix the location, how should it be designed? And perhaps even more critically, how do you decide which medicines to stock, and how much to keep on hand? In this chapter, we explore exactly that: how location, layout, and inventory planning come together to shape a pharmacy's success.

The location of a pharmacy is far more than a real estate decision. It determines footfall, prescription volume, visibility, and ultimately, profitability. When done right, it becomes the foundation for a thriving business. But a great location alone isn't enough. The design of the store, its layout, and lighting, zoning must serve both efficiency and customer comfort. Simultaneously, inventory planning ensures you carry the right mix of medicines to meet demand without overstocking or facing heavy expiry losses.

These three components, location, design, and inventory, are deeply interlinked. A pharmacy in a busy residential area may need different inventory compared to one near a hospital. A store layout optimized for walk-in healthy customers will differ from one built around chronic prescriptions. Knowing how to balance these elements requires both art and science.

Choosing High-Traffic or Prescription-Heavy Areas

Selecting the right site for a pharmacy can make or break the business. The ideal location is not just about rent or square footage; it's about understanding the behavior of the people around you and forecasting how they will use your store.

In many Indian cities, pharmacy owners instinctively gravitate toward high-traffic commercial streets, think near shopping areas, busy intersections, or bustling markets. This makes sense: more people walking by generally means higher walk-ins for over-the-counter (OTC) products. But that is only part of the story. A pharmacy near a hospital or clinic might attract fewer casual shoppers, but it often benefits from a steady flow of prescription patients. These customers are often loyal, return regularly, and generate consistent revenue.

Think of a pharmacy located just outside a network of clinics. Doctors refer patients right after consultation, and their prescriptions are filled immediately. By contrast, a downtown pharmacy in a commercial district may see bursts of foot traffic during lunch hours or weekends, with more impulse buys of wellness products, cosmetics, or basic OTC medicines. The footfall characteristics are very different, and so is the inventory mix that the pharmacy must maintain to serve its customer base.

For example, when evaluating potential locations for new branches, it is imperative to run a "prescription traffic vs. foot-traffic" analysis. One must study nearby general practitioners, polyclinics, and small clinics to estimate how many patients might come in requiring prescription fulfilment. Simultaneously, examine pedestrian counts, regional demographics, and local purchasing power to judge walk-in potential. The ideal site often emerges where these forces meet, a place with enough prescription volume to sustain reliable sales, and enough walk-in traffic to expand OTC and wellness margins.

Beyond pedestrian flow, parking, public transportation access, and visibility are critical. A store that is difficult to access or hidden behind other shops may suffer despite being in a busy region. In line with international design norms, good pharmacy location planning also considers accessibility for the elderly, people with mobility challenges, and even parents with young children. These customers are more likely to become regulars, provided the store is easy to reach.

Finally, real estate cost must be weighed against expected sales. High-traffic areas come with higher rents, but the incremental revenue from OTC sales and brand visibility may justify the cost. On the other hand, a prescription-heavy location with lower foot traffic might offer consistent margins, lower volatility, and deeper customer loyalty. Choosing the right trade-off requires a careful, data-driven assessment tailored to your business model.

Designing Efficient Layouts:
Zoning, Lighting, and Accessibility

Once the location is locked in, the next challenge is how to design the inside of the store. How you lay out shelves, counters, and zones can influence sales, customer experience, and staff productivity.

A thoughtful design begins with zoning: dividing the store into functional areas with purpose. One highly effective layout strategy is to place the prescription counter toward the back of the store. This may seem counterintuitive, but it is grounded in behavioral observation. Many shoppers, upon entering a store, turn right and begin walking counterclockwise, scanning familiar categories, wellness products, skincare, or OTC items, before reaching the pharmacy counter. Placing the prescription area at the end of this journey ensures customers walk past a variety of products. This not only optimizes product visibility but also encourages impulse purchases on the way.

Another design principle comes from well-established pharmacy layouts: combining a zoned and loop (racetrack) structure. This means the store is divided into clearly defined zones, for example, prescription drop-off, retail, wellness, and consultation, but the overall customer flow encourages a circular path around the store perimeter. This loop layout helps guide customers naturally, reducing congestion, enhancing discovery, and making navigation intuitive.

Lighting and accessibility matter just as much as zoning. Lighting has both functional and emotional roles. Ambient lighting creates a warm, welcoming atmosphere, while task lighting highlights specific product areas, like health supplements or acne treatment lines. Accent lighting can draw attention to featured displays or consultation zones, creating a sense of comfort and trust.

Accessibility is not optional, especially in community pharmacies. Wide aisles enable people with wheelchairs, walkers, or strollers to move freely. Counters should be designed with multiple heights, making it easier for elderly people or customers in wheelchairs to interact comfortably.

The counter, especially the pickup counter, is another critical design consideration. Research and design guides suggest placing impulse items like vitamins, travel-size OTC products, or health gadgets near the counter. This leverages the customer's waiting time to engage them and increase average basket size.

In some pharmacies, the back-of-house or staff workspace is separated from customer-facing zones, yet designed for efficiency. Pharmacists need easy access to stock, compounding areas, and computer systems; designers ensure that their workstations are ergonomic and logically placed, minimizing unnecessary movement. Experts stress that efficient layout improves workflow, reduces error rates, and supports better operational discipline.

All of these considerations emphasize that pharmacy design is not just about cosmetics; it is a deeply operational decision tied to customer flow, safety, transparency, and brand identity.

Inventory Classification: Chronic, Acute, OTC, Surgical

Inventory planning is the backbone of pharmacy profitability. Stocking the right categories of products ensures that you meet customer needs, manage cash flow, and minimize waste.

First, you need to understand how to classify inventory along key lines: chronic medications, acute-care drugs, over-the-counter (OTC) products, and surgical or medical supplies. Each category has different demand patterns, margins, and expiry risks.

Chronic medications, those for diabetes, hypertension, thyroid, and other long-term conditions, are the foundation of the prescription business. These drugs often generate consistent demand, month after month. Patients refill regularly, and they are likely to become repeat customers. For such items, the pharmacy must maintain a reliable buffer stock, and the reorder cycles should be relatively frequent but stable.

Acute-care drugs, like antibiotics, cold-and-flu medicines, and painkillers,see cyclical demand spikes. Their inventory strategy demands responsiveness: anticipate surges and fast-moving skews without overstocking. Here, data from past sales, prescribing trends, and even seasonal patterns play a crucial role.

Over-the-counter (OTC) products include vitamins, health supplements, self-care items, and common wellness goods. These typically have higher margins but are more sensitive to consumer trends and impulse purchasing. An effective OTC inventory strategy balances core staples (like analgesics) and rotating promotional or seasonal SKUs.

Surgical supplies, such as wound care items, disposables, and orthopedic supports, often sell more slowly but are essential for certain customers. While not all pharmacies have large surgical sections, those that do need to allocate shelf space wisely, forecast demand carefully, and monitor expiry closely, since some surgical products have limited shelf-life or must be reordered in small batches.

Inventory classification begins with sales analysis and customer segmentation. It is advisable to review prescription data, customer profiles, and footfall to decide how much shelf space goes to chronic, acute, OTC, and surgical categories. Then, set reorder thresholds: how many days of stock to maintain before reordering, taking into account lead times from distributors and our own usage patterns.

Implementing ABC (Always, Better, Control) analysis also helps. Try to categorize SKUs into high-turnover, medium-turnover, and low-turnover based on their contribution to sales and margin. This guides decisions on how frequently to reorder and how much safety stock to carry. For chronic drugs, for instance, we might keep a two-week buffer; for fast-moving acute drugs, we might reorder weekly, and for slower surgical items, we might keep a month's worth of inventory.

Another practical tool is using forecasting models that take past demand, lead times, and seasonal variations into account. For example, certain antibiotics may see a surge in the monsoon season, or allergy medicines may rise in the spring. Inventory planners use predictive analysis to forecast these demand changes and adjust orders accordingly.

Seasonal Demand Forecasting

Demand for medicines is not uniform throughout the year. Seasonal illnesses, festivals, and environmental changes drive predictable patterns, and smart pharmacies anticipate these fluctuations rather than react to them.

Consider the classic example of a pharmacy in North India. In the months of July to September, monsoon season brings an uptick in waterborne illnesses, flu-like infections, and gastrointestinal complaints. Sales of antacids, ORS (oral rehydration salts), antibiotics, and pain-relief medicines rise sharply. Conversely, in winter months, cough syrups, decongestants, and vitamin supplements typically see higher demand. Allergy medications may spike in spring or autumn.

But forecasting isn't just about weather. Local factors matter. For instance, a pharmacy located near a school or college may see more sales of painkillers and vitamins during exam seasons. A pharmacy close to a migrant community may experience changes during festival periods, as people return home or travel. Even public health campaigns, such as vaccination drives, can shift demand patterns dramatically.

A key insight from inventory science applies here: it is more cost-effective to hold slightly more stock for high-risk seasonal items than to face stock-outs when demand surges. For instance, ORS and antibiotic combinations may have lower margins, but if out of stock during a monsoon outbreak, patient loss and reputational risk are far greater.

At the same time, pharmacy teams must balance cash flow. Carrying too much seasonal stock ties up working capital and risks expiry. This is why inventory planners run scenario analyses, evaluating best-case, worst-case, and mid-case forecasts, and using that to decide reorder levels. They also rely on real-time sales monitoring so that if demand is lower than projected, they can adjust future orders to prevent overstock.

Visual Merchandising for Trust and Convenience

Visual merchandising is often associated with fashion or grocery retail, but in a pharmacy, it plays a deeply important role. It's not just about displaying products; it's about building trust, guiding customers, and ensuring a sense of safety and professionalism.

When a customer enters a pharmacy, the first few seconds matter. How the entrance looks, how products are arranged, and how signage is presented all shape the customer's perception. A clean, well-lit front with prominent displays of wellness products, seasonal items, or new customer-friendly brands sends a message: this is a place of care, expertise, and reliability.

Placing high-visibility items near the entrance or along the primary flow path helps. For instance, wellness displays, vitamins, self-care, and seasonal health products can be placed to the right of the entrance, where most customers naturally turn. Accent lighting on these displays draws the eye, making the store feel curated rather than cluttered.

At the counter area, merchandising should be subtle yet strategic. The counter isn't just where prescriptions are picked up; it's also a high-footfall space ideal for impulse items like small first-aid kits, baby care essentials, or travel-size health products. Well-placed shelving and neat baskets create options without overwhelming the customer.

Designing trust also means providing clarity. Clear signage, legible fonts, and calming color schemes all contribute. In some modern pharmacies, colored floor tiles or distinct visual cues guide customers from the entrance to the consultation area, prescription drop-off, and pick-up area. These pathways reduce confusion and help customers feel confident in navigating the space.

Consultation booths or private counseling areas, when integrated well, enhance the patient experience. By keeping them visibly accessible but separate enough to preserve privacy, pharmacies can encourage meaningful conversations between patients and pharmacists without compromising comfort or confidentiality.

Visual merchandising also involves flexibility. Shelving needs to be modular so stores can adjust arrangements based on seasonal trends, promotional cycles, or inventory changes. Moving shelves, adjusting height, or creating feature zones for high-margin or promotional items makes the space adaptable rather than static. This flexibility ensures the pharmacy remains relevant, responsive, and aligned with both business and patient-care goals.

Looking ahead, several trends are shaping how pharmacies think about location, design, and inventory.

One powerful trend is omnichannel integration. As digital orders grow, pharmacies increasingly design hybrid spaces that support both walk-in customers and order pick-up lockers or curbside delivery. This means that the layout must accommodate new touchpoints: dedicated zones for online prescription drop-off, storage bays for click-and-collect orders, and efficient back-of-store pathways.

Another trend is data-driven inventory planning. Advances in predictive analytics, AI, and machine learning are helping pharmacies forecast demand with greater accuracy. Techniques such as periodic-affine policies optimize stock levels in the face of uncertain demand, reducing waste and improving service.

Sustainable design is also gaining ground. Pharmacies are increasingly choosing eco-friendly shelving, energy-efficient lighting, and recyclable fixtures. Not only does this reduce environmental impact, but it resonates with customers who care about sustainability.

Moreover, customer experience is becoming healthcare experience. Pharmacies are transforming from mere dispensaries into wellness hubs. Flexible counseling spaces, digital health kiosks, and health workshop areas are part of emerging store concepts. As one design firm noted in their Delhi-based pharmacy projects, these stores are evolving to host health talks, vaccination camps, and wellness coaching, making the pharmacy a community center, not just a shop.

Finally, visual merchandising continues to evolve. Digital displays, interactive touchscreens, and smart shelving help personalize the in-store experience. Instead of static shelf tags, pharmacies can use digital signage to highlight promotions, provide health advice, and even suggest seasonal or locally relevant products.

References

- https://blog.ffb1.com/independent-pharmacy-layout-tips-to-improve-the-shopping-experience
- https://www.healthfacilityguidelines.com/ViewPDF/ViewIndexPDF/iHFG_part_b_pharmacy_unit
- https://www.alibaba.com/product-insights/pharmacy-store-design-layout.htm
- https://www.accessprojects.com.au/designing-customer-friendly-pharmacy-interiors/
- https://blog.ffb1.com/independent-pharmacy-layout-tips-to-improve-the-shopping-experience/
- https://www.alibaba.com/product-insights/pharmacy-store-design-layout.html
- https://www.iyubocustom.com/pharmacy-counter-design-guide/
- https://www.shreedesigns.in/hospital-pharmacy-design
- https://www.shreedesigns.in/hospital-pharmacy-design
- https://en.wikipedia.org/wiki/Visual_merchandising
- https://www.iajps.com/wp-content/uploads/2024/02/68.IAJPS68012024.pdf
- https://www.scribd.com/document/367666382/74893970-Pharmacy-Layout-Design
- https://arxiv.org/abs/1806.06744

Chapter 6

Procurement & Vendor Management

Procurement is the quiet engine of every pharmacy retail operation. It does not stand at the storefront, does not greet customers, and does not appear in marketing campaigns, yet it determines something far more fundamental: whether a pharmacy can serve its community without interruption. Behind every medicine on a shelf lies a long chain of decisions, negotiations, and relationships. Most people outside the industry never see this world, yet it is the backbone that keeps the business functioning every single day.

For anyone running a pharmacy retail chain in India, procurement is not a simple task of ordering stock. It is a living system influenced by the behaviour of manufacturers, the operational realities of distributors, the unpredictability of demand, the seasonal variation in illnesses, and the complex dynamics of credit, returns, margins, and supply chain risks. The larger a chain grows, the more the procurement function shifts from ad-hoc buying to a structured discipline that must be planned, documented, and continuously monitored.

When a pharmacy achieves stable procurement practices, everything downstream becomes steadier. Margins improve, expired stock reduces, working capital frees up, store teams breathe easier, and customers experience consistent availability. When procurement is mismanaged, even the most beautifully designed stores and well-trained pharmacists struggle to compensate for empty shelves, frozen cashflows, or inconsistent supplier behaviour. In this chapter, we take a deep, practical walk through the everyday reality of procurement and vendor management in Indian pharmacy retail, not from a theoretical angle, but through what actually happens behind closed doors.

Building Relationships With Pharma Companies and Distributors

The pharmaceutical supply chain in India operates on relationships. Technology, portals, digital invoicing, and automated indenting have entered the picture, but the heart of the system still relies on trust built over conversations, visits, and consistency in daily dealings. A procurement team that can cultivate strong relationships with suppliers will always have an advantage over one that depends purely on transactions.

Most pharmacies begin their relationship journey with distributors. Manufacturers typically work with stockists or super distributors who handle supply across cities or districts. For a pharmacy chain, the relationship with the local distributor is crucial because daily operations rely on them. It is the distributor who ensures whether your store receives medicines on the same day, next morning, or sometimes not at all. A strong relationship can mean faster deliveries, priority allocation of limited-availability medicines, better credit terms, and occasional support during crises.

The relationship itself is built slowly. Every time a procurement manager calls to adjust an indent, request an urgent item, or dispute a short supply, the interaction either strengthens trust or weakens it. There are distributors who will push everything aside to help a pharmacy that they have worked with for years. There are others who function strictly by rules. Both types exist in the market, and procurement teams must learn to navigate their personalities just as much as the products they supply.

With manufacturers, the relationship is slightly different. While distributors handle daily supply, companies focus on larger agreements such as rate contracts, promotional schemes, bulk deals, and strategic partnerships. When a pharmacy chain grows to a certain size, companies begin to notice. Medical representatives and area managers make regular visits, and over time, category managers, regional heads, and procurement officers sit across meeting tables to negotiate annual plans.

These meetings can influence an entire year of procurement. The conversation may begin with basic introductions and end with an agreement covering bonuses, targets, quarterly schemes, co-branding possibilities, or even exclusive rates. What determines the outcome is not only the size of the chain but also how professionally the pharmacy presents itself. Manufacturers appreciate clarity. When a pharmacy produces clean reports, predictable order volumes, and transparent selling patterns, companies are far more willing to extend support.

In this environment, strong vendor relationships are not built by chance. They require a mix of professionalism, patience, and consistency. Prompt payments, clear communication, and straightforward resolution of disputes build long-term goodwill. Vendors talk among themselves, and reputation travels faster than most retailers realise. A pharmacy chain known for honouring commitments will find doors opening automatically.

Credit Cycles, Negotiation, and Return Policies

One of the most sensitive aspects of procurement is managing credit. The credit cycle in pharmacy retail can determine whether a business has free working capital or whether it is constantly stressed. Most distributors offer 15 to 30 days of credit depending on the relationship, the order volume, and the reputation of the retailer. A well-established chain may receive 45 days, and in rare cases, 60 days, especially for high-volume purchases.

Credit can be a blessing when managed well and a trap when misused. When stores place orders without tracking cashflows, the entire chain finds itself stuck with pending payments. Distributors begin restricting supply, medicines run short, and store managers start scrambling to meet customer needs. This ripple effect comes from one simple misalignment: excess dependence on credit without aligning it to real sales.

Negotiation enters the picture here. Many new entrepreneurs assume negotiation means simply asking for higher margins or more discount. But distributors operate on extremely thin spreads. They are bound by manufacturer guidelines, market competition, and their own expenses. A skilled procurement manager negotiates holistically. Instead of pushing for more margin, the conversation focuses on better payment terms, additional credit days, improved return flexibility, early settlement incentives, or faster delivery cycles.

Some negotiations revolve around schemes. Companies often run offers such as buy ten and get one free, quarterly bonuses tied to purchase volumes, or seasonal promotions. A retailer who understands which schemes align with actual demand is able to make informed choices rather than accumulating excess stock.

Return policies are another area where experience makes a difference. Every pharmacy faces the challenge of expired medicines. Although modern inventory systems reduce the risk, no store can eliminate expiry completely. The distributor's willingness to accept returns, particularly near-expiry items, becomes a major relationship factor. Some distributors strictly accept returns only before the last month of expiry. Others allow returns up to the second last month. A few support the retailer fully and consider returns throughout the shelf life, provided the quantities are reasonable.

Having a clear, mutually accepted return policy saves tension later. Retailers who send back excessive quantities without justification often face friction. Those who manage stock responsibly and return only unavoidable items usually receive better cooperation. Over time, vendors perceive which retailers value the relationship and which ones treat it only as a chance for negotiation.

Supplier Performance Tracking and Risk Mitigation

In a small store, the owner often knows which distributor is reliable simply from experience. But in a chain with dozens or hundreds of outlets, procurement must become systematic. Vendor performance cannot be judged by memory alone. It requires disciplined tracking.

The broader purpose of tracking supplier performance is not to police vendors but to create a predictable environment for the chain. A store manager should know that when he places an order, the medicines will arrive within a certain time, without discrepancies, in proper packaging, and with correct billing. When this consistency breaks, operations start falling apart.

The most common parameters used for assessing suppliers include fill rate, delivery speed, accuracy in billing, consistency of schemes, responsiveness to complaints, and willingness to support in emergencies. Fill rate is particularly important. It measures what percentage of the ordered items were supplied. A distributor who supplies only half the items will force a store to raise multiple small orders, which increases operational load and often results in stockouts.

A procurement team often maintains a vendor scorecard. It does not have to be a complex dashboard. Even a simple monthly summary highlighting which distributor delivered consistently and which one producedprodkuced too many shortages can help decision makers. Over time, these scorecards guide larger negotiations, especially when deciding which vendors will handle bulk commitments.

Risk mitigation also plays a central role here. A pharmacy chain is vulnerable to multiple types of risks: supply disruption, regulatory non-compliance, distributor defaults, natural disasters, unexpected shortages, or sudden spikes in demand. Many of these risks cannot be eliminated, but they can be reduced.

For supply disruption, the best mitigation strategy is maintaining alternative vendors. No large chain depends entirely on one stockist for any critical category. A second distributor or a backup supply channel ensures continuity. In high-demand seasons, some chains even build small safety stocks across key items like paracetamol, ORS, cough syrups, and antibiotics.

Another area of risk is quality. With India's large number of pharmaceutical manufacturers, the risk of receiving substandard or improperly stored items increases. Procurement teams must be cautious about buying from unfamiliar vendors offering unusually high margins. Every year, regulatory authorities publish alerts on substandard medicines. A reputable chain cannot afford to stock products without proper verification.

Some risks are more subtle. For instance, if a supplier consistently sends short-dated items without disclosing it, the store may be forced to sell aggressively or risk expiry. A procurement manager who monitors shelf life at the time of receiving can identify such patterns early and address them before they become recurring issues.

All these practices together ensure that the supply chain remains stable even when market conditions fluctuate.

Inventory Forecasting and Technology Tools

Inventory forecasting has become one of the most crucial parts of procurement because customer behaviour is changing. People expect instant availability. They compare prices across platforms. They shift brands based on doctor prescriptions, reviews, or familiarity. Seasonal illnesses behave differently each year. A chain that forecasts poorly ends up with blocked capital or chronic stockouts.

The old style of procurement depended heavily on gut feeling. Many store owners developed a sense of what moved fast, what needed replenishment, and what required discounting. Their experience was valuable but limited to one store. For a chain, forecasting must be scientific.

Modern pharmacy chains rely on sales pattern analysis. They examine which products sell consistently every month. They track chronic medicine movement, which forms a large part of recurring sales. They analyse seasonal spikes during monsoon, winter, and summer. A good forecasting system also studies store location. A pharmacy near a hospital behaves differently from one in a residential area.

Technology tools have made forecasting easier. Some chains use simple tools like Excel to map sales trends. Others invest in cloud-based inventory management systems that automatically suggest reorder points. Advanced platforms analyse store wise demand and place automated indents whenever stock drops below a threshold.

Technology is helpful, but it works best when paired with real-world judgment. For instance, an algorithm may recommend stocking more of a particular antibiotic based on last month's sales. A procurement manager who keeps track of local medical patterns may know that these sales were influenced by one hospital's temporary prescription preference. When that pattern shifts, demand falls. Human judgment recognises this nuance.

Forecasting is also important for negotiation. A chain that understands its own demand can negotiate bulk rates confidently. It can commit to quantities without risking overstock. This turns procurement into a proactive function rather than a reactive one.

Technology also helps with batch tracking. Barcode scanning, batch-wise alerts, and expiry notifications reduce losses and improve return success. During audits, digital records make compliance smoother.

Stores no longer depend on manual checking of expiry dates, which reduces human error.

Some chains integrate forecasting with centralised warehouses. This allows them to buy in bulk at better rates, store items centrally, and distribute them to individual stores. Warehouse based models require stronger forecasting because the risk of accumulating slow moving stock increases. But when executed well, it leads to higher margins and more stable supply.

The Human Side of Procurement

Behind all the systems, policies, and negotiations, procurement is still a human function. It involves judgement, relationships, experience, and intuition. A procurement manager develops a certain instinct over time, a kind of internal alarm system that activates when something feels off. It may be a distributor suddenly changing behaviour, a manufacturer altering schemes, or a supplier pushing an unusually high quantity of one product.

Human experience plays an irreplaceable role. For example, there are situations where everything looks fine on paper, but the procurement team senses that a particular supplier might struggle to deliver consistently. Perhaps deliveries have become erratic, or invoices contain small mistakes. These small patterns often reveal larger operational weaknesses. Technology alone cannot catch these subtleties.

Another human element is empathy. Vendors are also running businesses. They have their own pressures, delays, audits, and cashflow challenges. A chain that treats vendors with respect earns loyalty. During crises, this loyalty becomes invaluable. There are real stories of distributors prioritising certain retailers during medicine shortages simply because of years of trust and goodwill.

Procurement teams that maintain professionalism while also understanding the human context build stronger partnerships. In the Indian pharmacy environment, this balance is essential. Too much rigidity damages relationships. Too much flexibility damages the business. The art lies in finding the middle ground.

The Future of Procurement in Indian Pharma Retail

Procurement in pharmacy retail is gradually evolving. As the industry grows more organised, vendors are becoming more structured, distributors more transparent, and manufacturers more collaborative. Chain pharmacies are adopting centralised procurement models, automated indenting, and real-time inventory tracking.

E-pharmacies have pushed the entire sector toward digitisation. Their ability to analyse large amounts of data has influenced how physical retailers think about demand forecasting. Even small standalone pharmacies are now adopting basic software to track stock movement.

In the coming years, procurement will likely see greater use of predictive analytics. Weather data, disease patterns, and hospital admission reports may begin influencing forecasting models. Digital platforms that connect retailers with multiple distributors through a single interface may become common.

Yet, even with all this technological progress, procurement will always retain a human core. Decisions made across a table, a shared understanding between retailer and distributor, and the instinct developed through years of experience will remain irreplaceable.

A chain that learns to combine technology with human judgement will always stay ahead.

References

- https://cdsco.gov.in
- https://nppa.gov.in
- https://pharmexcil.com
- https://www.researchgate.net/publication/308890011_Distribution_Structure_in_Indian_Pharmaceutical_Industry_Significance_of_Customer_Relationship_Management_CRM_and_Distributor_Relationships
- https://www.dolcera.com/wiki/index.php?title=Indian_Pharma_Industry_-_Distribution_%26_Sales_Force_Structure
- https://www.scribd.com/document/81786093/Pharma-Distribution-System-India
- https://rklifecare.com/blog/the-role-of-drug-distributors-in-a-pharma-company
- https://www.intellistride.com/blog/the-role-of-fda-and-cdsco-guidelines-in-indias-cold-chain-logistics-safety/
- https://www.credenceresearch.com/report/india-retail-pharmacy-market
- https://www.cci.gov.in/images/marketstudie/en/market-study-on-the-pharmaceutical-sector-in-india1652267460.pdf

Chapter 7

Hiring and Training Pharmacists & Staff

Pharmacy retail ultimately rests on people. Systems, technology, and supply chains enable efficiency, but the quality of care experienced by a patient depends on the individuals who operate the store each day. Hiring and training are therefore not operational afterthoughts. They are foundational decisions that shape safety, compliance, reputation, and long-term sustainability.

Unlike many retail formats, a pharmacy employs professionals who work at the intersection of healthcare delivery and commercial execution. The responsibility carried by pharmacy staff is significant. Errors have clinical consequences, regulatory implications, and ethical dimensions. This reality requires a disciplined approach to recruitment, structured training, and continuous performance development. The objective is not simply to fill roles, but to build a team capable of delivering consistent, compliant, and patient-centered service.

This chapter examines how pharmacy retailers can approach workforce building with rigor and foresight. It addresses the skills and qualifications required, clarifies core store roles, outlines practical training and compliance mechanisms, emphasizes the importance of communication and empathy, and explores strategies to retain and motivate staff over time.

Skill Sets and Qualifications

Defining the skill sets and qualifications for pharmacy staff is the first critical step in ensuring quality care and operational safety. Skill requirements in pharmacy practice combine formal education, professional credentials, technical competence, ethical understanding, and situational judgment. These diverse elements must be mapped thoughtfully to each role in the pharmacy team.

Formal Education and Professional Credentials

For pharmacists, formal education is highly regulated because of the direct impact their work has on patient safety. In many countries, including India, an accredited Diploma in Pharmacy (D.Pharm) or Bachelor of Pharmacy (B.Pharm) degree is the minimum education requirement. These programs cover rigorous coursework in pharmaceutical sciences, pharmacotherapy, medicinal chemistry, dose calculation, pharmaceutical law, and practical lab work. Graduates must then register with the relevant pharmacy council or regulatory authority to practice legally. This licensing process confirms that individuals have met defined standards of knowledge and are accountable to professional regulation.

Globally, the Doctor of Pharmacy (PharmD) degree has become the standard in many developed healthcare systems. The PharmD program integrates clinical application, direct patient care experiences, case-based learning, and advanced therapeutics. These programs also emphasize interprofessional collaboration, preparing graduates to work alongside physicians, nurses, and other healthcare professionals in complex care environments.

Pharmacy assistants and technicians may not require the same level of formal education, but structured training remains crucial. Many regions offer accredited certificate or diploma programs that introduce pharmacy terminology, inventory systems, basic pharmacology, and the legal framework for pharmacy operations. Even when formal certification is not mandatory in a jurisdiction, employers increasingly prioritize candidates who have completed accredited training because it reduces onboarding time and ensures baseline competence.

For cashiers and store managers, the educational expectations are usually focused on business, retail operations, or customer service fundamentals. However, employers should still verify that candidates understand data privacy requirements, basic healthcare compliance, and the importance of confidentiality in pharmacy settings.

Technical Competence: Beyond Knowledge to Application

Technical competency in pharmacy is more than memorizing drug lists or understanding dosage tables. It is the skill of applying knowledge safely, consistently, and accurately. For pharmacists, this includes the ability to:

- Evaluate the appropriateness of prescriptions for therapeutic efficacy and safety.
- Identify potential drug interactions, contraindications, and duplicate therapies.
- Adjust counseling approaches for patients with varying health literacy levels.
- Manage controlled substances with strict adherence to legal and ethical standards.
- Participate in clinical activities like medication therapy management when applicable.

Technical competence for assistants and technicians involves precision, consistency, and procedural reliability. These professionals manage shelf stocking, label preparation, inventory reconciliation, prescription assembly for verification, and support logistical operations. Their work is essential to the efficiency and safety of the dispensing process. Even without making clinical judgments, their tasks require meticulous attention to detail because errors at this stage may propagate into patient harm if not intercepted.

Technical competence also includes digital skills. Pharmacy management software, electronic databases, bar-coding systems, and point-of-sale interfaces are core tools of everyday work. Fluency with these systems improves efficiency and reduces errors that occur when staff struggle with manual processes or outdated technology.

Regulatory Awareness and Ethical Responsibility

Pharmacy staff operate in one of the most highly regulated areas of healthcare. Staff must understand regulatory obligations related to drug storage, documentation retention, reporting requirements, adverse event follow-up, and controlled drug handling.

Ethical responsibility is inseparable from regulatory compliance. Staff must respect patient confidentiality, act with integrity in financial transactions, report errors transparently, and avoid conflicts of interest. Ethical lapses in pharmacy work can erode patient trust, compromise safety, and expose practices to legal liabilities.

Standards of professional conduct are usually defined by national pharmacy councils or boards. Employers should ensure that new hires are aware of these standards and that performance evaluations explicitly include ethical conduct and regulatory knowledge.

Behavioral and Professional Attributes

Technical skills can be taught. Professional attributes such as reliability, teamwork, adaptability, effective communication, and response under pressure are personality traits that often determine long-term success in patient-facing healthcare roles.

During recruitment, behavioral interviews that explore how candidates respond to complex problems, manage conflict, and support teamwork can reveal these soft but vital qualities.

In pharmacy practice, these attributes support quality, consistency, and a culture of shared responsibility.

Roles: Pharmacist, Assistant, Cashier, Store Manager

A high-performing pharmacy is a well-coordinated human system. Each role brings distinct responsibilities, boundaries, and opportunities for impact. Clarity in these roles supports effective teamwork, reduces error, and aligns expectations across the organization.

Pharmacist

The pharmacist is the clinical authority of the pharmacy. They are the most senior clinical professional on duty and carry the legal responsibility for anything that touches patient care. Their core duties include:

- Verifying prescription integrity and clinical appropriateness.
- Assessing potential risks such as drug interactions or allergies.
- Providing medication counseling that supports therapeutic adherence.
- Interpreting diagnostic information when available and communicating with other healthcare providers when needed.
- Overseeing the work of assistants and technicians, ensuring that all delegated tasks meet regulatory and quality standards.
- Managing controlled medication storage, tracking, and reconciliation.

In essence, pharmacists act as the final checkpoint in the medication use process. They protect patients by combining technical knowledge with real-time judgment and clear communication.

Pharmacy Assistant and Technician

Pharmacy assistants are essential operational partners to pharmacists. They facilitate workflow efficiency and create capacity for pharmacists to focus on clinical tasks. Assisted responsibilities typically include:

- Preparing prescriptions for verification by pharmacists.
- Managing inventory including stock rotation and expiry monitoring.
- Supporting customer service for routine queries and directing clinical questions appropriately.
- Maintaining a clean, organized, and compliant work environment.
- Supporting documentation and record-keeping for regulatory audits.

Technicians often assume responsibilities beyond those of assistants, depending on jurisdictional regulations. Technicians may manage delegated steps in dispensing under formal protocols, handle order entry with greater autonomy, and participate in quality assurance processes. Targeted training and ongoing competency assessment ensure that these roles support safe dispensing while remaining within legal scope.

Cashier

The cashier role extends beyond financial transactions. In many patients' experiences, the cashier is the first and last human contact they have in the pharmacy. Their duties include:

- Processing payments accurately.
- Handling refunds and billing reconciliations with professionalism.
- Upholding patient confidentiality during interactions.
- Recognizing inquiries that require pharmacist involvement and responding with appropriate escalation.
- Managing customer expectations with courtesy and clarity.

While not clinical, the cashier's role influences patient satisfaction, trust, and how safe and respected patients feel during their visit.

Store Manager

The store manager is responsible for operational excellence and workforce oversight. This role integrates business performance with the demands of regulated healthcare delivery. Responsibilities include:

- Overseeing staffing, scheduling, and workload balance.
- Managing inventory, suppliers, and logistics.
- Ensuring compliance with regulatory documentation, record retention, and audit readiness.
- Leading performance evaluations, coaching, and professional development.
- Implementing systems that support continuous improvement in safety, quality, and patient experience.

Store managers translate organizational policy into everyday practice. Their leadership shapes workplace culture, operational resilience, and the ability to adapt to regulatory or market changes.

Training Programs and Compliance Checks

Train staff inadequately, and even the most qualified recruit underperforms. Training is much more than orientation. It is a sustained, structured, and documented process that integrates people into safe practices and supports ongoing competence.

Onboarding: The First Step to Competence

Onboarding is often undervalued. A comprehensive onboarding program sets expectations, introduces team culture, and begins the journey toward independent competence. Onboarding includes:

- Orientation to workplace technology, protocols, and safety procedures.
- Introduction to quality systems and reporting structures.
- Assignment of mentors who guide new staff in real workflows.
- Checklists that track a new hire's progress toward core competencies.

For example, an assistant entering day one might complete an inventory management tutorial, observe prescription preparation procedures, and begin supervised practice. This structured introduction accelerates confidence and reduces early errors.

Role-Specific and Continuing Training

Training must be dynamic. Pharmacy staff work in environments where regulatory changes, new therapies, and patient needs evolve continuously. Well-designed training programs include:

- Core clinical training for pharmacists in areas such as medication therapy management, new drug approvals, and updated therapeutic guidelines.
- Structured practical workshops for assistants on inventory software, prescription labeling protocols, and accuracy checks.
- Customer interaction training for cashiers that emphasizes confidentiality, escalation protocols, and professionalism.
- Leadership development for managers that includes compliance interpretation, audit readiness, and performance coaching.

Training should balance knowledge acquisition with practical application. Microlearning modules, team simulations, and supervised practice build both competence and confidence.

Competency Assessment and Compliance Audits

Training is meaningful only if it translates into performance. Competency assessment is a systematic evaluation of whether staff can perform their roles safely, consistently, and in compliance with regulations. These assessments include:

- Observed practice evaluations.
- Knowledge checks or quizzes following training modules.
- Documentation audits ensuring record accuracy and retention.
- Reconciliation of controlled medications as required.

Routine compliance audits help identify gaps, reinforce standards, and protect the pharmacy from regulatory findings. Regular feedback loops ensure that training is updated based on audit results and workplace observations.

Incident Reporting and Safety Culture

A mature training environment includes systems for reporting errors, near misses, and concerns. Incident reporting systems are designed not to punish individuals but to improve systems. Staff must trust that reporting leads to analysis, corrective action, and shared learning. Root cause analysis frameworks help teams examine incidents collaboratively and reduce recurrence.

Soft Skills and Patient Empathy in Communication

Technical competence alone does not define quality pharmacy practice. Much of the value that patients receive from pharmacy services lies in how staff communicate, listen, and engage with empathy.

Patient-Centered Communication

Patients often arrive at a pharmacy with uncertainty, fear, or confusion about their health. Effective patient-centered communication includes:

- Active listening to understand concerns before responding.
- Use of plain language that patients can understand.
- Confirmation of understanding through methods like teach-back.
- Nonjudgmental responses that put patients at ease.

Effective communication is not an innate skill for everyone. It can be taught, practiced, and reinforced through role-plays, feedback sessions, and reflection.

Empathy as a Core Professional Skill

Empathy is not synonymous with sentimentality. Instead, it is the ability to recognize patient emotions, validate experiences, and respond in ways that respect dignity. Empathy supports clinical outcomes by increasing trust and improving adherence to medication instructions. Regular training to develop empathy strengthens staff confidence in handling emotionally charged conversations.

Cultural Awareness and Inclusivity

Pharmacies serve diverse communities. Cultural humility and sensitivity training help staff communicate respectfully across differences in language, belief systems, and health practices. Inclusive communication promotes access and reduces disparities in care.

Staff Retention and Motivation Practices

Hiring top talent is only half the challenge. Retaining them is equally, if not more, difficult. Staff turnover disrupts workflow, increases costs, and diminishes patient experience. Implementing evidence-based retention strategies creates stability and organizational resilience.

Competitive Compensation and Transparent Rewards

Fair and transparent compensation structures remain foundational to retention. Competitive salaries, clear pay bands, and pathways for increases based on performance and competencies signal respect and value for staff contributions.

Career Growth and Professional Development

Staff are more likely to remain engaged and loyal when they see opportunities for growth. Structured career pathways, access to advanced training, professional certifications, and support for continuing education nourish long-term retention.

Workplace Culture and Leadership Support

A positive workplace culture with supportive leadership influences staff satisfaction more than perks do. Managers who listen, recognize achievements, and engage staff in decision-making cultivate trust and performance.

Routine "stay conversations" where leaders ask about aspirations, challenges, and support needs reveal early insights that prevent turnover. These proactive conversations strengthen relationships and identify opportunities to improve workplace systems.

Work-Life Balance and Wellbeing Practices

Pharmacy work can be demanding. Rotating schedules, sustained high volume, and emotional labor contribute to burnout if left unmanaged. Policies that support flexible scheduling, adequate staffing levels, breaks, and access to wellbeing resources create healthier workplaces.

Recognition and Engagement Programs

Recognition is a powerful motivator. Celebrating achievements, acknowledging contributions publicly, and creating systems of appreciation reinforce positive behaviors. Engagement programs such as employee-suggestion forums and quality circles involve staff in continuous improvement and deepen ownership in outcomes.

The journey from hiring to developing a thriving pharmacy workforce is intentional and multifaceted. It requires clarity of roles, rigorous training systems, empathy in communication, and evidence-based retention strategies. Organizations that invest strategically in their people build safer, more effective, and more trusted pharmacy services. When patients encounter staff who are competent, confident, and compassionate, the entire healthcare experience is elevated.

Pharmacy leaders who embrace workforce development not as an administrative requirement but as a core organizational priority establish not just great workplaces, but healthier communities.

Building a pharmacy team is a long-term investment. Recruitment decisions shape culture. Training practices determine reliability. Leadership behavior influences morale. Together, these elements define how a pharmacy functions under routine conditions and during moments of stress.

Pharmacies that prioritize people alongside systems create environments where accuracy, empathy, and accountability coexist. Such environments benefit patients, protect regulatory standing, and sustain commercial performance.

In the evolving landscape of pharmacy retail, human capability remains the most enduring differentiator.

References

- https://www.randstad.in/job-seeker/job-profiles/pharmacy-assistant
- https://www.the-pda.org/wp-content/uploads/education-training-requirements-pharmacy-support-staff-june-2019.pdf
- https://www.ahrq.gov/es/health-literacy/pharmhealthlit/pharmlit/pharmtrain.html
- https://pubmed.ncbi.nlm.nih.gov/40034876
- https://pharmaceutical-journal.com/article/letters/using-stay-conversations-to-improve-retention-and-staff-experience-among-specialist-pharmacists
- https://www.who.int/teams/patient-safety
- https://www.who.int/teams/health-workforce

Chapter 8

Technology and Automation in Retail Pharmacy

In the day-to-day of a pharmacy, technology might not be the first thing a customer notices when they walk in. A patient's focus is on the friendly greeting they receive, the pharmacist's advice, or the reassurance that their medicine is in stock. But behind the scenes, technology quietly orchestrates many of the systems that make this level of service possible. In the competitive and regulated world of pharmaceutical retail, technology and automation have become indispensable. They shape how pharmacies manage inventory, interact with customers, run billing operations, maintain compliance, and prepare for the future.

Technology in pharmacy retail is not a luxury; it is the backbone of modern operations. Without it, pharmacies would be unable to keep pace with the demands of inventory management, regulatory compliance, customer engagement, and supply chain logistics. Patients today expect faster service, accurate stock availability, seamless billing, and personalised care. These expectations have driven retail pharmacies to adopt systems that go well beyond cash registers and paper logs. The evolution of technology in this sector reflects a broader shift in retail: from manual processes to integrated, data-driven operations.

POS Systems, Billing, and Smart Inventory Management

The point of sale, or POS system, is where the business of the pharmacy meets the customer. Years ago, a POS system might have been little more than a cash register and a basic ledger, but in today's pharmacies, it has evolved into a powerful hub that does much more than process payments. Modern POS technology integrates billing, inventory tracking, customer history, regulatory checks, and even compliance features into one interface.

Think of a typical day in a mid-sized pharmacy. A customer walks in with a prescription for multiple medicines. The pharmacy staff uses a smart POS system to scan each item. In a fraction of a second, the system not only processes the sale but also checks stock levels, updates inventory counts, verifies tax calculations, and records the transaction against the customer's purchase history. If one of the medicines requires a prescription, the system flags it automatically and prompts the staff to upload or note the prescription details. This level of integration reduces human error and ensures that every sale is compliant and traceable.

Billing through such systems has become more than simply calculating totals and printing a receipt. A POS system today is a data engine. It captures sales patterns, gives insights into which products are fast-moving, and identifies seasonal or periodic demand changes. These insights help pharmacies plan better for future purchases, avoid stock outs, and minimise wastage. A well-implemented POS system becomes a decision support tool, not just a billing machine.

What makes modern POS systems particularly valuable in pharmacy retail is their ability to link billing with inventory in real time. In the past, pharmacies had to reconcile sales ledgers with inventory logs at the end of the day or week. This manual reconciliation was time-consuming and prone to errors. Today, as soon as a product is invoiced at the counter, the inventory count adjusts automatically. Managers can open a dashboard and see stock levels across the store, know which SKUs are running low, and make purchase decisions with confidence. The automation of billing and inventory provides clarity and reduces the mental load on staff who previously juggled multiple logbooks.

Software providers have also introduced pharmacy-specific features such as controlled drug monitoring and audit trails in POS systems. These features help ensure that pharmacies comply with regulatory needs for documentation, especially for drugs with specific sales requirements. All this happens without slowing down the service experience for the customer.

Stock Alerts, Expiry Tracking, and Automated Purchase Orders

Inventory management is the heartbeat of a pharmacy. Medicines are perishable, with expiry dates that must be monitored closely. A misplaced batch sitting past its expiry not only represents a financial loss but also a potential risk to patient safety. It is here that technology truly changes the game.

Let us consider a scenario. In a pharmacy that uses manual logs, expiry dates might be tracked on paper or spreadsheets. Staff members might check shelves periodically, but human limitations can lead to oversight. Stock alerts may be ignored, and a batch could expire before it is removed from inventory or sold at a discount. This kind of loss is not uncommon in traditional pharmacy settings.

Smart inventory systems transform this process. These systems maintain detailed records of every item's batch number, expiry date, and purchase history. They constantly monitor the stock, and when a product is approaching its expiry, the system generates alerts. These alerts can be sent to multiple stakeholders—the store manager, the pharmacist in charge, or the procurement team. Early warning allows the pharmacy to take action, such as offering discounts to clear stock, returning products to vendors where policy allows, or even redistributing stock to branches where demand exists.

In addition to expiry tracking, modern systems can detect low-stock levels and generate automatic purchase orders based on pre-defined thresholds. For example, if a particular antibiotic is a fast mover in the store and its quantity falls below a set point, the inventory system can automatically prepare a purchase order for approval. This removes the need for manual intervention and ensures that the pharmacy does not run out of critical medicines. Pharmacies that rely on automated purchase orders often report a dramatic reduction in stockouts and improved cash flow because they avoid overstocking slow-moving items.

Another advantage of automated systems is the tracking of purchasing patterns over time. By analysing historical data, these systems can forecast future demand with reasonable accuracy. This capability is invaluable during periods of predictable spikes, such as flu seasons or pre-festive demand surges. A pharmacy that knows it is entering flu season can proactively stock antipyretics, cough syrups, and influenza treatments well in advance, thanks to forecast models within inventory software.

A truly advanced system also accounts for expiries and order cycles together. Suppose an item has only a few months left before expiry but remains in reasonable demand. A smart inventory tool will flag this and recommend either expedited promotions to clear the inventory or suggest smaller order quantities for future cycles to avoid repetition. This level of optimisation was almost impossible when tracking was manual.

In addition to expiry and restocking, these systems streamline communications with suppliers. Rather than placing phone calls or sending emails, automated purchase orders can be sent dirctly to approved vendors with specifics on batch size, expected delivery date, and price terms. This speeds up procurement and reduces the administrative burden on pharmacy staff.

CRM, Mobile Apps, and Loyalty Programs

Technology in pharmacy retail does not stop at inventory and operations. It extends into the heart of customer engagement and long-term relationship building. In a crowded retail environment, pharmacies can no longer rely on location or word of mouth alone. They need strategies that personalise the experience, reward loyalty, and build repeat business. This is where Customer Relationship Management, or CRM systems, mobile apps, and loyalty programs become vital.

A CRM system for a pharmacy captures and manages customer data in a way that fosters ongoing engagement. It stores contact information, purchase histories, prescription trends, and preferences. When used thoughtfully, CRM tools allow pharmacists to personalise communications. For example, a pharmacy can send a gentle reminder to a patient that their chronic medication refill is due, or inform them of an upcoming health camp or discount event.

Mobile apps have become a powerful extension of CRM systems. A customer who downloads a pharmacy's app gains access to prescription uploads, order tracking, refill reminders, and exclusive offers. Instead of relying solely on a walk-in visit, patients can interact with the pharmacy digitally. They can view their purchase history, check medicine prices, and receive alerts when a prescription is about to expire or require renewal.

Loyalty programs are another technology-driven tool that strengthens customer relationships. Similar to loyalty cards used in other retail segments, pharmacy loyalty programs can reward customers with points for purchases, referrals, or adherence to refill schedules. These points can then be redeemed for discounts, free health checkups, or wellness products. Over time, such programs help convert occasional buyers into regular patrons.

CRM systems can also segment customers based on behaviour, health needs, or purchase frequency. A CRM might identify patients who buy diabetes medications regularly and send them targeted content on diet plans or community health events focused on diabetes management. This type of personalised engagement increases the value customers associate with the pharmacy beyond the transactional level.

Mobile apps further enhance accessibility. They can integrate with digital wallets, offer secure payment options, and allow customers to request home delivery—a feature that has become especially important in urban areas and among elderly patients. Apps also collect data that can be analysed to improve service offerings. For instance, if data shows that a large percentage of users prefer delivery during evenings, the pharmacy can adjust its delivery schedules to match customer preferences.

Loyalty programs designed with empathy and utility, not just discounts, tend to perform best. A pharmacy might offer customised wellness packages based on a patient's life stage—maternity care packages for expecting mothers, bone health supplements for seniors, or child immunisation reminder bundles. These programs tap into customer needs and provide value that goes beyond price reductions. The technology that supports these programs ensures that benefits are tracked accurately and applied consistently across purchase channels, whether in-store or through a mobile app.

For example, Artificial Intelligence, or AI, is no longer just a futuristic term in retail pharmacy. It is being integrated into operations in ways that enhance accuracy, forecasting, and customer engagement. One compelling example of AI's application is in inventory forecasting and prescription processing.

In several modern pharmacy chains, AI tools analyse historical sales data along with external factors such as seasonal trends, public health alerts, and even weather patterns to predict demand for specific medicines. These predictive models become more accurate over time as they ingest more data. For example, if a pharmacy chain notices that cough suppressants and antihistamines surge every year before the monsoon season, AI can automatically alert procurement teams to stock higher quantities ahead of time. This proactive approach reduces stockouts and improves patient satisfaction.

AI is also being used to streamline prescription processing. Machine learning algorithms can scan uploaded prescriptions, interpret handwritten notes, and identify medicine names with improving accuracy. In crowded pharmacies where multiple customers arrive simultaneously with prescriptions, this capability can dramatically reduce waiting times and errors. Some AI tools cross-verify prescriptions against drug interaction databases, flagging potential concerns for pharmacists to review. This safety net is invaluable, especially in high-volume settings.

Another area where AI shows promise is in customer engagement. Chatbots integrated with pharmacy mobile apps can answer common questions, provide information on store hours, give medication instructions, and even schedule delivery slots. While these chatbots do not replace human pharmacists, they free up staff time by handling routine queries, allowing pharmacists to focus on patient counselling and complex interactions.

Large pharmacy chains have also experimented with AI-driven dynamic pricing for over-the-counter wellness products. By analysing demand, competitor pricing, stock levels, and seasonal variations, AI models can suggest optimal pricing that balances sales volume with profitability.

One real-world example of AI integration is a large Indian retail pharmacy chain that implemented an AI-powered demand forecasting system. The system consolidated sales data from hundreds of outlets, incorporated regional health trends, and generated automated stock recommendations for each store. As a result, the chain reduced wastage due to expiry by significant percentages and improved in-stock percentages for fast-moving products. While the initial investment in AI tools was substantial, the long-term gains in operational efficiency, customer satisfaction, and reduced deadstock made the investment worthwhile.

What makes AI particularly valuable is its capacity to learn and adapt. Unlike static rule-based systems, AI algorithms become smarter with more data. They can detect patterns that might elude human analysts and respond to real-time changes in demand. In an industry where both overstocking and stockouts have financial and patient-care consequences, this level of intelligence becomes a powerful differentiator.

Human-First View of Technology and Automation

Throughout all these technological innovations, one thing remains clear: the human element is still central. Technology does not replace pharmacists; it empowers them. When a pharmacist uses a POS system to quickly pull up a patient's medication history, the interaction becomes more personalised and informed. When inventory systems handle routine tracking of expiry dates and purchase orders, pharmacists have more time to focus on counselling patients and addressing complex queries. When mobile apps send reminders to patients about refills, adherence improves, contributing to better health outcomes.

Technology amplifies human skills and compassion. It removes drudgery, reduces errors, supports decision-making, and enhances customer engagement. A smartly automated pharmacy is not cold and impersonal; it is efficient, empathetic, and responsive to patient needs. For patients with chronic illnesses, technology means reminders, easier order placements, and fewer chances of missing medications. For pharmacy staff, it means less time navigating paperwork and more time connecting with customers on matters of health and wellness.

A fully tech-enabled pharmacy feels modern and seamless to the customer. Yet, behind that seamless experience sits an intricate web of systems working in harmony—POS systems processing transactions with accuracy, inventory tools ensuring shelves are stocked wisely, CRM systems building relationships that extend beyond transactions, and AI tools anticipating needs before they arise.

Historically, pharmacies were manual, paper-driven environments where records were kept in ledgers and orders were placed over the phone. Today, they are dynamic centres of healthcare powered by data, automation, and intelligent systems. The transformation is not just operational; it is cultural. It reflects a shift toward patient-centric care, where technology supports the human mission of wellness and healing.

In the years ahead, automation will continue to evolve. AI will become more integrated into clinical support, predictive care models, and personalised health journeys. Mobile platforms will offer deeper engagement, linking pharmacy care with broader health ecosystems. Analytics will drive smarter procurement, better pricing strategies, and improved adherence programmes. But at every step, the goal will remain unchanged: to make the pharmacy experience smoother, safer, and more meaningful for patients and providers alike.

Technology and automation are not ends in themselves. They are tools that help pharmacies deliver on their promise of care and reliability. A pharmacy that embraces technology with empathy and professionalism offers more than medicines; it offers confidence, continuity, and care that patients can count on.

References

- https://www.softwareadvice.com/retail/pharmacy-management-software-comparison/
- https://arxiv.org/abs/2506.11011 (inventory management research) (arXiv)
- https://www.retailcustomerexperience.com/articles/how-pharmacy-retailers-are-using-technology/
- https://www.gartner.com/en/insights/crm
- https://builtin.com/artificial-intelligence/ai-healthcare
- https://www.ibef.org/industry/pharmaceutical-india.aspx
- https://blog.nalashaahealth.com/top-features-of-pharmacy-inventory-management
- https://www.swindia.com/swil-blog/how-ai-is-transforming-the-pharmacy-retail-sector
- https://antavo.com/blog/pharmacy-loyalty-programs/

Chapter 9

Store Operations and Standard Operating Procedures

A pharmacy may have the right location, competitive pricing, and a recognisable brand, but without disciplined store operations, everything else eventually collapses. Store operations are where strategy stops being aspirational and becomes real. They determine whether a pharmacy feels dependable or erratic, whether customers trust the counter instinctively or second-guess every transaction, and whether regulators view the store as compliant or constantly questionable.

In pharmaceutical retail, operations carry a responsibility that far exceeds ordinary retail execution. Pharmacies are not merely points of sale; they are extensions of the healthcare delivery system. They influence treatment continuity, patient adherence, medication safety, and public trust in the broader healthcare ecosystem. Errors here are not limited to financial loss or momentary dissatisfaction. They can affect health outcomes, delay recovery, worsen chronic conditions, or expose vulnerable patients to harm. This reality places an ethical obligation on pharmacy operators to run stores with exceptional discipline.

Standard Operating Procedures (SOPs) exist to fulfil this obligation. They are often misunderstood as documents created for inspectors, auditors, or corporate checklists. In practice, SOPs are behavioural frameworks. They define how people act when the store is crowded, when systems are slow, when staff is short, or when ambiguity arises.

They replace inconsistency with clarity and ensure that safety does not depend on memory, mood, or individual interpretation.

SOPs also make growth possible. A single pharmacy can function on informal supervision and the owner's constant presence. A chain cannot. As operations expand across locations, people rotate, experience levels vary, and local pressures differ. Only well-designed SOPs ensure that quality, safety, and compliance remain intact regardless of who is on duty or which store a customer walks into.

This chapter examines store operations in a structured and balanced manner. It explores daily, weekly, and monthly SOPs in depth, along with cash control, inventory discipline, audit preparedness, cleanliness, documentation, safety checks, and the challenge of maintaining consistency across multiple stores. Each section is treated with equal importance because pharmacy operations are systemic: weakness in any one area eventually affects the whole.

Daily Store SOPs

Daily SOPs form the operational foundation of a pharmacy. They govern how the store opens, functions, serves customers, manages medicines, and closes. Their strength lies not in complexity but in consistency. When daily routines are followed with discipline, they prevent small lapses from accumulating into serious compliance or safety issues.

In most pharmacies, major failures rarely occur suddenly. They develop quietly through repeated shortcuts—missed temperature checks, delayed system entries, hurried substitutions, or undocumented decisions. Daily SOPs exist to interrupt this pattern. They create a rhythm of checks and balances that keeps operations aligned with standards, even during peak hours.

Store Opening Procedures

Store opening is an operational reset. The condition in which a pharmacy opens sets expectations for staff and customers alike. A late opening, technical confusion, or visible disorganisation immediately erodes credibility and creates avoidable stress.

Pharmacies often serve customers early in the morning who depend on medicines for chronic or life-sustaining conditions. For these patients, medicine availability is not a convenience but a necessity. Opening discipline therefore becomes part of patient care.

Operating hours must be followed strictly. Opening routines should be standardised rather than left to individual preference. Electrical systems, computers, POS terminals, printers, barcode scanners, billing software, and internet connectivity should be activated in a fixed sequence. This reduces system errors and ensures readiness before customer interaction begins.

A short buffer period after opening should be reserved for internal checks. During this time, staff verify cash float availability, review pending online or telephonic orders, check refrigerator temperatures, and ensure counters and dispensing areas are clean and organised. Rushing directly into billing without preparation often leads to errors that disrupt the entire day.

Cleanliness checks are integral to opening SOPs. Counters, shelves, storage units, refrigerators, dispensing trays, and waiting areas must be inspected visually. In a pharmacy, cleanliness is interpreted as safety. Customers may not understand pharmacology, but they instinctively associate order and hygiene with trustworthy medicine handling.

Mandatory licenses and certificates must be prominently displayed and periodically reviewed for validity and legibility. These include the drug license, pharmacist registration certificate, and other statutory approvals. Their visibility reassures customers and signals regulatory seriousness during surprise inspections.

The registered pharmacist must be present, identifiable, and active during operating hours. This role is not symbolic. The pharmacist anchors ethical dispensing, prescription validation, patient counselling, and regulatory compliance from the very start of the day.

Inventory and Stock Management

Inventory in a pharmacy is both financial capital and patient dependency made physical. Each strip, vial, or bottle represents continuity of therapy and trust in availability. Poor inventory practices compromise both business viability and patient care.

Daily checks should prioritise fast-moving and essential medicines, especially those linked to chronic therapies such as diabetes, hypertension, asthma, thyroid disorders, and cardiac conditions. Repeated stock-outs in these categories quietly push customers toward competing pharmacies, often permanently.

Temperature-controlled inventory demands uncompromising discipline. Refrigerators must be checked daily, and temperature logs reviewed rather than mechanically filled. Staff should understand that these records protect medicine efficacy, not just regulatory compliance. Vaccines, insulin, biologicals, and certain ophthalmic preparations are especially sensitive to deviations.

Expiry management is a daily responsibility. Near-expiry medicines should be identified early, segregated clearly, and labelled visibly. They must never remain mixed with regular stock. Many compliance failures arise not from deliberate wrongdoing but from poor segregation during busy periods.

All inward receipts, sales, and returns must be updated in the POS system in real time. Delayed entries distort inventory visibility, confuse replenishment planning, and create audit discrepancies. Accuracy at the point of transaction prevents cumulative operational confusion.

Prescription Handling and Dispensing

Prescription handling is the most critical function of a pharmacy. It is the moment where operational discipline directly intersects with patient safety.

Every prescription must be reviewed carefully and deliberately. The pharmacist should verify prescriber credentials, date validity, dosage instructions, duration, and therapeutic logic. Unclear handwriting, unusual combinations, or dosing inconsistencies should be clarified rather than assumed.

Dispensing must strictly follow the prescription. Where substitutions are permitted, they must be communicated transparently. Patients should understand what medicine they are receiving, why a substitution was made, and how it affects their therapy. Confusion undermines trust even when clinical equivalence exists.

Patient counselling is a professional responsibility. Clear guidance on dosage timing, food interactions, storage conditions, and precautions prevents misuse and adverse outcomes. Counselling does not require lengthy explanations, but it does require attention, empathy, and clarity.

Compliance with Schedule H, H1, and X regulations must be absolute. Registers must be updated immediately and accurately. Documentation shortcuts taken during peak hours often become serious liabilities during inspections.

Customer Service and Billing

A pharmacy counter is often a place of vulnerability. Customers arrive anxious, unwell, or under financial stress. Staff behaviour must reflect this reality.

Respectful communication, patient listening, and calm explanations are core operational skills, not optional niceties. They influence trust as much as medicine availability.

Billing accuracy is non-negotiable. Customers should clearly understand what they are being charged for and why. Errors in billing create suspicion that can extend to doubts about medicine authenticity and ethical practices.

Generic alternatives should be introduced responsibly. Customers must be informed about therapeutic equivalence and price differences without pressure or judgement. Ethical guidance builds long-term loyalty.

Complaints must be handled professionally and without defensiveness. Each complaint is operational data, highlighting gaps in process, communication, or training. Pharmacies that respond constructively convert complaints into trust.

Cash and Compliance Checks

End-of-day reconciliation ensures financial integrity. Cash, UPI, card settlements, and POS reports must align exactly. Discrepancies should be investigated immediately while details are still fresh.

Cash, controlled-drug documentation, and sensitive records must be secured according to protocol. Digital data should be backed up daily. Data loss is not merely an IT issue; it is an operational and compliance failure.

Closing SOPs must be followed methodically. Electrical equipment should be powered down safely, refrigerators checked, controlled stock secured, and all entry points locked. A disciplined close enables a calm and efficient opening the next day.

Weekly Store SOPs

Weekly SOPs shift operations from reactive execution to reflective control. They allow the store to analyse patterns, correct inefficiencies, and strengthen discipline before issues escalate.

Stock Review and Replenishment

Weekly sales analysis reveals trends that daily views cannot. Fast-moving items, seasonal spikes, and emerging therapy categories become visible. This insight allows more accurate replenishment planning.

Slow-moving and dead stock must be reviewed honestly. Excess inventory blocks working capital and increases expiry risk. Weekly review enables timely corrective actions such as stock transfers, supplier returns, or discount-led liquidation.

Critical medicines require zero-tolerance stock-out policies. Consistent availability defines pharmacy reliability more strongly than pricing or promotions.

Quality and Compliance Audit

Weekly internal audits reinforce discipline. Prescription registers, statutory documentation, temperature logs, and storage practices should be reviewed systematically.

Issues identified internally are easier to correct and far less costly than regulatory penalties. Routine audits build inspection readiness without creating fear or disruption.

For chain pharmacies, brand compliance and SOP adherence should also be reviewed weekly to maintain uniformity across locations.

Housekeeping and Visual Merchandising

Weekly deep cleaning prevents gradual deterioration of hygiene. Shelves, storage units, refrigerators, and dispensing areas must be cleaned thoroughly.

Visual merchandising should remain responsible and current. Outdated posters, damaged signage, or misleading promotions should be removed. Order and clarity communicate professionalism without words.

Team Review and Training

Weekly team reviews align people with processes. Attendance, punctuality, and workload distribution should be discussed transparently.

Short refresher training sessions reinforce SOPs and address recurring errors. Regular reinforcement builds muscle memory and reduces dependence on individual recollection.

Monthly Store SOPs

Monthly SOPs focus on reconciliation, strategic alignment, and long-term sustainability. They convert operational data into managerial insight.

Inventory and Financial Reconciliation

Monthly physical stock audits reconcile system data with reality. Discrepancies must be analysed deeply to identify root causes such as pilferage, billing errors, or receiving lapses.

Sales performance, margins, expiry losses, and shrinkage trends should be reviewed in detail. These insights inform procurement strategies, pricing decisions, and operational improvements.

Structured reports should be submitted to management or head office to enable central oversight and benchmarking.

Regulatory and Documentation Review

Licenses, renewals, and statutory records must be reviewed monthly for validity and completeness. Pharmacist attendance records and professional certifications should be updated and filed systematically.

Regulatory readiness achieved through routine discipline is far more robust than last-minute preparation.

Vendor and Supply Chain Review

Supplier performance directly affects medicine availability and service quality. Monthly reviews help address delivery delays, shortages, damages, and return efficiency.

Credit terms, outstanding balances, and payment cycles should be monitored to maintain healthy cash flow and stable supplier relationships.

Performance and Compliance Review

Monthly reviews must balance financial targets with operational discipline. Targets achieved through shortcuts create long-term risk.

Corrective actions should follow every review. Documentation without execution weakens operational credibility and erodes accountability.

Preventive Maintenance

Preventive maintenance reduces breakdowns and compliance risk. Refrigerators, POS systems, CCTV, electrical fittings, and internet connectivity should be checked regularly.

Data backups and cybersecurity reviews ensure continuity and protect sensitive information from loss or misuse.

Ensuring Consistency Across Multiple Stores

Consistency is the ultimate test of operational maturity. SOPs, training, audits, and technology must work together to create uniform experiences across locations.

Consistency does not mean rigidity. Local adaptation is healthy and often necessary. However, core safety, ethical, and compliance standards must never vary. Successful chains clearly define what is non-negotiable and what can be adapted.

Importance of Cleanliness, Documentation, and Safety Checks

Cleanliness in a pharmacy is not cosmetic; it is foundational. Documentation is not paperwork; it is accountability. Safety checks are not formalities; they are tools for risk prevention.

Together, these elements create operational integrity. A pharmacy that is clean, well-documented, and safety-conscious earns trust quietly—from customers, regulators, doctors, and partners alike.

Pharmacy operations are not sustained by intention alone. They are sustained by discipline, repetition, and clarity. SOPs translate values into daily action and ensure that safety, ethics, and quality are upheld even under pressure.

A well-run pharmacy does not depend on heroic effort or constant supervision. It depends on systems that guide behaviour, protect patients, and support staff. When SOPs are designed thoughtfully and followed consistently, they create stability, trust, and scalability.

In an environment of increasing regulatory scrutiny, rising patient expectations, and intense competition, disciplined store operations are no longer optional. They are the foundation upon which sustainable pharmacy businesses are built.

References

- https://cdsco.gov.in/opencms/opencms/en/Home/
- https://pharmacycouncil.nic.in/content/education-regulations

- https://www.mohfw.gov.in/
- https://www.fip.org/good_pharmacy_practice
- https://www.fip.org/publications
- https://www.who.int/teams/health-product-policy-and-standards
- https://www.who.int/publications/i/item/WHO-TRS-961
- https://www.who.int/medicines/areas/quality_safety/quality_assurance
- https://www.who.int/initiatives/medication-without-harm
- https://www.sciencedirect.com/topics/pharmacology-toxicology-and-pharmaceutical-science/pharmacy-practice
- https://academic.oup.com/jpp
- https://www.tandfonline.com/toc/ijpp20/current https://www.who.int/publications/i/item/WHO-IVB-15.04
- https://www.who.int/publications/i/item/WHO-TRS-1025
- https://www.cdc.gov/vaccines/hcp/admin/storage/toolkit/storage-handling-toolkit.pdf
- https://www.unicef.org/supply/cold-chain-equipment
- https://www.who.int/tools/prequalifications

Chapter 10

Marketing in Pharma Retail

Marketing in pharmaceutical retail occupies a distinctive position within the broader landscape of consumer marketing. Unlike conventional retail categories, where marketing is often designed to stimulate impulse purchases, amplify desirability, or push seasonal demand, pharma retail marketing operates within the boundaries of healthcare ethics, patient safety, and regulatory compliance. The core product being sold is not a lifestyle accessory; it is often a therapy, a continuation of treatment, or a necessity that directly affects a person's wellbeing. Consequently, effective pharmacy marketing is not built on persuasion alone. It is built on trust, continuity, accessibility, and responsible communication.

A modern retail pharmacy is expected to do more than dispense medicines. Customers increasingly approach pharmacies for advice on minor ailments, guidance on OTC selection, basic monitoring (blood pressure checks, glucose checks), and support for chronic therapy adherence. In many communities, the pharmacy is the most accessible healthcare touchpoint, visited more frequently than clinics or hospitals. Marketing, therefore, cannot be treated as a standalone "promotion function." In pharma retail, marketing is an extension of operations and service quality. A pharmacy that consistently stocks essential medicines, dispenses accurately, counsels responsibly, and resolves complaints professionally is already conducting its strongest form of marketing, because it is building reputational equity in the neighbourhood.

At the same time, competitive intensity has risen sharply. Customers compare prices, demand home delivery, and expect digital convenience. Regional chains and national players create awareness through branding, loyalty programs, and omnichannel presence. E-pharmacy and online aggregators further shape expectations by offering convenience and discounts. In such an environment, pharmacies, whether independent or chain-operated, must market strategically to remain visible and relevant. However, the most sustainable marketing approaches are those that align with the pharmacy's healthcare role rather than attempt to imitate FMCG-style retail promotions.

This chapter examines marketing in pharma retail through a structured and professional lens. It focuses on (i) local marketing methods such as pamphlets, WhatsApp campaigns, and community engagement; (ii) brand-building through digital channels; (iii) doctor engagement, health camps, and preventive healthcare initiatives; (iv) loyalty and retention strategies; and (v) a real-world case study demonstrating how a leading pharmacy retailer used loyalty, data, and health-focused initiatives to build long-term growth. The chapter concludes with practical principles and verified reference links.

Marketing Objectives in Pharma Retail

Before discussing tactics, it is important to clarify what marketing should achieve in a pharmacy context. In most retail categories, the primary marketing goals are awareness, acquisition, and conversion. In pharma retail, those goals remain relevant, but they are insufficient on their own. Pharmacies must prioritise an additional set of outcomes that directly connect to healthcare delivery and customer trust.

Trust and Credibility as the Central Marketing Asset

For a pharmacy, trust functions as the most valuable brand equity. Customers evaluate a pharmacy not only on price but on perceived safety:

- Are the medicines authentic?
- Is the pharmacist present and attentive?
- Are substitutions transparent and ethical?
- Does the store handle prescriptions responsibly?
- Are errors acknowledged and corrected quickly?

Trust is built through consistent behaviour. Marketing can accelerate awareness, but it cannot compensate for weak service quality. In fact, aggressive marketing with weak operations can backfire, attracting new customers who quickly churn due to poor experience, leaving negative reviews and reputational damage.

Convenience and Continuity of Care

Pharmacy purchases are often recurring, especially for chronic therapies. Marketing, therefore, must support continuity. A pharmacy that helps customers refill on time, offers home delivery, confirms stock availability quickly, and maintains a clean, dependable store experience will retain customers more effectively than a pharmacy that relies solely on discounts.

Convenience-based marketing in pharmacy includes:

- Refill reminders and adherence support
- Home delivery with reliable timelines
- Quick digital ordering (WhatsApp, app, call)
- Clear, transparent billing
- Consistent availability of chronic medicines

These features reduce friction and make the pharmacy a default choice.

Responsible Value Communication

Value in pharma retail should not be reduced to "cheap medicines." Customers do value affordability, but they also value:

- Correct pack sizes and avoidance of unnecessary purchases
- Ethical generic alternatives with clear explanation
- Accurate guidance on OTC selection
- Bundling for chronic care essentials (e.g., glucometer strips, BP monitor accessories)
- Loyalty benefits that reduce long-term cost without encouraging irrational consumption

Pharmacy marketing must communicate value without overpromising outcomes or encouraging inappropriate medicine use.

Brand Positioning in a Local Healthcare Ecosystem

A pharmacy competes not only with other pharmacies, but also with:

- e-pharmacy delivery platforms
- Clinic-attached dispensaries
- Hospital pharmacies
- Neighbourhood "medical stores" that operate informally

Strong pharmacy brands position themselves as:

- Reliable and professional
- Available and responsive
- Ethically guided and patient-friendly
- Integrated with preventive health habits

This positioning becomes the foundation on which local marketing, digital presence, and loyalty programs can be built.

Local Marketing: Pamphlets, WhatsApp Campaigns, and Community Engagement

Local marketing is often the highest-return marketing category for independent pharmacies and regional chains. It leverages proximity and everyday visibility. The objective is to become the pharmacy that customers remember first, especially for chronic refills and family needs, rather than the pharmacy they find only in emergencies.

Pamphlets and Local Print Collateral

Pamphlets remain effective in many Indian neighbourhoods, particularly where:

- Residential density is high (apartment clusters, societies)
- Clinic footfall is significant
- Elders and families dominate the demographic
- Digital discoverability is still developing

However, pamphlets only work when designed and distributed with discipline.

Content Principles for Pharmacy Pamphlets

A pharmacy pamphlet should focus on service clarity, not promotional exaggeration. Recommended content includes:

- Store name, address, landmark, and operating hours
- Ordering options (call/WhatsApp)
- Service offerings: home delivery, refill reminders, chronic care support, availability checks
- Categories: chronic medicines, OTC, personal care, diabetic supplies, baby care, elderly care
- Trust signals: pharmacist availability, licensed store, authentic medicines assurance
- Compliance note: "Prescription required for prescription medicines"

Design and Readability

Pharmacy customers value clarity more than creativity. Simple design, readable font sizes, and neat category blocks often outperform crowded discount posters. A pamphlet should be easy to scan in 10 seconds.

Distribution Strategy

Effective distribution is targeted rather than random:

- Apartment societies (with permission; ideally in collaboration with RWA)
- Near clinics: reception placement or patient handouts (ethical, non-intrusive)
- Diagnostic centres (especially where people purchase follow-up medicines)
- Local grocery stores, salons, or community hubs (cross-placement works)

What to Avoid

Pharmacies should avoid pamphlets that:

- Promote prescription-only medicines in a promotional tone
- Make "guaranteed cure" or exaggerated claims
- Encourage self-medication for serious conditions
- Mimic FMCG-style persuasion that undermines healthcare credibility

Pamphlets should function as a "service introduction," not a hard sale.

WhatsApp Campaigns and Service Communication

In many parts of India, WhatsApp has become the most practical "digital layer" for neighbourhood pharmacies. Its advantage lies in familiarity: customers do not need to download an app, learn a system, or create an account. For pharmacies, WhatsApp can become an operating channel (orders, delivery, reminders) and a marketing channel (service awareness, seasonal education) simultaneously.

The correct approach: utility-first messaging

The effectiveness of WhatsApp marketing depends on whether customers perceive it as service or spam. The most sustainable model is to treat WhatsApp as a patient support channel and use marketing sparingly. Below are some high-impact WhatsApp use cases

Prescription Photo Ordering

1. Customers send a prescription image; the store confirms availability and bill amount; delivery or pickup is arranged.
2. **Monthly refill reminders**
3. For chronic patients: "Your monthly refill is due. Reply YES for home delivery."
4. **Stock availability updates**
5. Especially during shortages: confirmation messages that reduce patient anxiety and unnecessary trips.
6. Delivery coordination
7. Address confirmation, timing, payment mode, and substitution clarification (where permitted).
8. Seasonal preventive messages
9. Monsoon fever prevention tips, hydration reminders, allergy season guidance, kept educational, not promotional.

Best Practices for Compliance and Privacy

- Use WhatsApp Business for labels, quick replies, and structured workflows.
- Obtain consent for reminders and broadcast lists.
- Limit frequency of broadcasts.
- Protect privacy: never share customer medical details in group messages; avoid public exposure.
- Use neutral language: service updates and education rather than aggressive selling.

Simple WhatsApp campaign templates (professional tone)

- "Refill Reminder: Your monthly medicines are due this week. Reply 1 for home delivery, 2 for pickup."
- "Service Update: Home delivery available in [localities] between [hours]. Prescription required for prescription medicines."
- "Seasonal Advisory: During monsoon, ensure safe drinking water and hydration. For persistent fever, consult a doctor."

Used responsibly, WhatsApp becomes a retention engine. It keeps the pharmacy present in the customer's routine without reducing the relationship to discounts.

Community Engagement as Trust Marketing

Community engagement is not the fastest marketing channel, but it is among the most durable. A pharmacy that becomes known as helpful, stable, and educational earns loyalty that discount competitors struggle to break.

Community engagement formats that work

- Senior citizen support: priority billing line, monthly monitoring reminders, assistance with medicine organisers
- Apartment society sessions: "safe medicine storage at home," "BP basics," "diabetes adherence checklist"
- School/community first-aid awareness (non-commercial)
- Women's health education sessions: anemia awareness, calcium/vitamin D education (ethically presented)
- Seasonal awareness: hydration drives, dengue prevention information sessions, antibiotic course completion education

What makes community engagement successful

- **Sincerity:** Customers must feel it is truly helpful
- **Professionalism:** Avoid sensational claims and avoid playing the role of "doctor substitute"

- **Collaboration:** Partner with a qualified professional for camps where needed
- **Continuity:** Repeating small programs builds recognition more than one big event

In pharma retail, community engagement is best viewed as reputation infrastructure.

Brand-Building and Awareness Through Digital Channels

Even a local pharmacy now operates in a digital discovery environment. Customers search online before visiting, especially in urban areas. Digital presence is not about "influencer marketing." It is about discoverability, credibility, and consistency.

Google Business Profile as a Primary Brand Surface

For most pharmacies, Google Business Profile (GBP) is the most important digital marketing asset. Customers search phrases like:

- "pharmacy near me"
- "medical store open now"
- "home delivery pharmacy"
- "insulin available nearby"

A complete and active GBP improves visibility and reduces customer uncertainty. Below is a core optimisation checklist

- Accurate name, address, phone number, hours
- Updated holiday timings
- Clear service descriptions: home delivery, refill reminders, availability checks
- Clean, recent photographs (storefront, counter, aisles, pharmacist area)
- Review management: encourage satisfied customers to review; reply to feedback professionally

- Weekly updates: health camps, seasonal advisories, service announcements

Reviews act as social proof. In healthcare-adjacent retail, customers often trust reviews as strongly as recommendations from neighbours.

Social Media for Education and Local Familiarity

Social platforms (Instagram, Facebook) work best for pharmacies when used for:

- Health awareness content
- Service visibility
- Local familiarity ("this pharmacy is active, professional, and clean")

Content categories suited to pharmacy channels

- Safe storage reminders (heat, monsoon)
- OTC selection basics (non-prescriptive): ORS, antacids, pain relief precautions
- Device guidance: inhaler technique awareness, glucometer usage tips (high-level)
- Preventive care reminders: hydration, seasonal allergies, mosquito control
- Compliance reminders: "prescription required for prescription medicines"

Local growth strategy

- Location tagging and local hashtags
- Community partnerships (gyms, dietitians, clinics) with ethical boundaries
- Photo documentation of health camps (with consent)
- Staff professionalism highlights (pharmacist presence, counselling desk)

Social media should not attempt to replace professional consultation. Its role is to reinforce pharmacy credibility and approachability.

A Simple Website or Landing Page for Credibility

A pharmacy does not require a complex website to benefit from digital presence. Even a single-page site improves:

- Search ranking
- Professional legitimacy
- Service clarity (delivery, hours, ordering process)

A basic page should include:

- Contact details and map
- Hours and delivery zones
- Services offered
- Compliance disclaimer on prescription medicines
- Privacy reassurance for customer data

Paid Digital Advertising: Service-led and Compliant

Paid ads can be effective when used for:

- Announcing delivery service areas
- Promoting extended hours
- Advertising health camps or BP check drives
- Highlighting "chronic refill support" services

Ads should avoid promoting prescription medicines directly or making health claims. In healthcare-related advertising, restraint strengthens trust.

Doctor Connects, Health Camps, and Preventive Healthcare Drives

Pharma retail marketing becomes significantly more effective when it integrates into the local healthcare ecosystem. This does not mean unethical inducement or influencing prescribing. It means building professional credibility and supporting patient continuity.

Doctor Connect Programs (Ethical and Professional)

A doctor connect strategy in pharmacy should be designed around patient support:

- Consistent availability of commonly prescribed medicines
- Accurate and ethical dispensing
- Reliable substitution communication (where permitted)
- Respectful handling of prescriptions
- Pharmacist availability for queries

When doctors trust a pharmacy's dispensing discipline, they feel confident that patients will be served responsibly. That trust can indirectly increase pharmacy preference among patients, without unethical behaviour.

Health Camps as Outreach and Relationship-Building

Health camps can deliver three outcomes simultaneously:

- Community value
- Brand visibility
- Customer retention pipeline (especially chronic customers)

Camp formats commonly used

- Blood pressure checks
- Blood glucose screening (with correct protocols)
- BMI and basic lifestyle guidance (non-prescriptive)
- Inhaler technique awareness sessions
- Medication adherence counselling sessions for seniors

Execution standards

- Qualified supervision where needed
- Hygiene and consent

- Responsible handling of personal data
- Referral guidance rather than diagnosis claims
- Follow-up messaging focused on support (refill reminders, monthly monitoring), not aggressive selling

Health camps are among the most ethically acceptable marketing tools because they contribute to preventive health and position the pharmacy as a health partner.

Preventive Healthcare Drives

Preventive initiatives build long-term brand identity. These include:

- Antibiotic course completion education
- Safe self-medication awareness
- Seasonal fever prevention communication
- Chronic adherence reminders ("don't stop medicines without doctor advice")
- Elder medicine safety (polypharmacy awareness, storage guidance)

When done consistently, such drives create a "health-first" brand perception that supports sustainable growth.

Loyalty Programs and Customer Retention Strategies

Pharmacy retail is structurally well-suited for loyalty, because many purchases recur monthly. However, loyalty in pharmacy is not created by points alone. It is created by the combination of habit + trust + convenience.

Principles of a Pharmacy Loyalty Program

A pharmacy loyalty program must be:

- Simple to understand
- Easy to execute at billing

- Transparent in redemption
- Designed around repeat behaviour and service value

Common models:

- Points per purchase with redeemable value
- Membership programs with service benefits (delivery, priority billing)
- Family accounts linked to one number
- Chronic care support plans (refill scheduling + small benefits)

In pharmacy retail, benefits that reduce friction (delivery, reminders) often outperform pure discount points.

Retention Mechanisms Beyond Points

The strongest retention drivers are operational:

- Dependable stock of chronic medicines
- Refill reminders and proactive communication
- Fast grievance resolution
- Patient counselling quality
- Predictable delivery timelines
- Accurate billing and clear substitutes

A retention strategy should be designed as a system. Loyalty points may be one part of it, but the foundation must be operational excellence.

Customer Segmentation for Ethical, Relevant Communication

Segment customers to avoid blanket promotions:

- Chronic therapy patients: refill reminders, monthly monitoring offers
- Seniors: delivery support, counselling emphasis

- Young families: baby care essentials, vaccination-related OTC guidance (non-prescriptive)
- Acute buyers: seasonal preventive tips
- Wellness buyers: safe supplementation education

Segmentation enables relevance without excessive messaging.

Measuring Retention in Pharma Retail

A pharmacy should measure:

- Repeat purchase rate (monthly cohorts)
- Refill adherence (for enrolled chronic customers)
- Average time between purchases
- Delivery adoption rate
- Complaint resolution time
- Review growth and sentiment

Marketing without measurement becomes guesswork. Ethical marketing requires proof that campaigns improve service and retention rather than merely generate noise. Boots is among the most established pharmacy-led health and beauty retailers in the UK. Over decades, it has developed strong consumer loyalty through a long-running membership program, the Boots Advantage Card, and has increasingly used its loyalty ecosystem to support both commercial performance and health-oriented initiatives.

This case is relevant to pharma retail marketing because it demonstrates how a pharmacy retailer can build growth through loyalty, value positioning, and data-led personalisation, without reducing marketing to discount banners alone.

Marketing Challenge

Retail pharmacy environments face common challenges:

- Consumers expect value and convenience
- Competitors compete aggressively on pricing

- Health and beauty categories are increasingly digital
- Trust and reputation remain crucial due to healthcare association

Boots responded by strengthening its loyalty proposition and using customer relationships built over many years to make communications more relevant and service-oriented.

Strategy: Loyalty as a Core Marketing Engine

Boots has historically invested in loyalty as a long-term relationship mechanism. Public reporting and marketing commentary indicate that loyalty growth has been an important driver of customer engagement and sales performance. For example, Boots reported growth in active Advantage Card membership, with reporting indicating over 16.9 million active members and a quarterly increase tied to sign-ups and loyalty engagement.

Rather than positioning loyalty purely as "points," Boots has increasingly linked loyalty to value propositions and personalised offers. Commentary also highlights how Boots leverages its long Advantage Card history to enhance personalisation and customer relevance in marketing.

Execution: Data-Led Personalisation and Contextual Marketing

A particularly instructive element is how Boots has been recognised for using data to adjust marketing contextually. A Campaign Tech Awards write-up described Boots being commended for data-driven marketing linked to contextual triggers (e.g., reacting to pollen data and media placements).

For pharma retail marketing, this illustrates a practical principle: campaigns can be built around real customer needs and seasonal health context rather than generic promotions.

Health-First Engagement Through Loyalty Infrastructure

Boots' own reporting also provides an example of using loyalty infrastructure in health-related initiatives. In an ESG/impact report, Boots described engagement through Advantage Card in the context of identifying individuals potentially at risk in a study environment.

While not a "marketing campaign" in the traditional sense, this demonstrates how a pharmacy retailer can use its customer relationship systems to support health initiatives, strengthening brand trust and purpose.

Results and Learning for Pharma Retail

This case offers several transferable lessons for pharmacy marketing (including Indian retail pharmacy contexts):

- Loyalty must be positioned as service value, not only points.
- When loyalty supports convenience (personalised offers, relevant reminders, value framing), it becomes habit-forming.
- Personalisation increases relevance and reduces promotional fatigue.
- Generic discount messages are easily ignored; context-driven communication tied to seasonal health needs has stronger engagement.
- Trust-first brands can compete beyond price.
- When customers feel a pharmacy understands their needs and supports their wellbeing, they become less price-sensitive over time.
- Health initiatives strengthen brand legitimacy.
- Pharmacy retailers have an opportunity to contribute to preventive health, which builds deep reputational equity.

For independent and regional pharmacies, the Boots case does not imply that sophisticated data systems are mandatory. Instead, it highlights an approach: build a customer relationship framework (even through simple systems like WhatsApp + refill enrolment + basic loyalty), then use that framework to communicate service, value, and preventive care consistently.

Marketing in pharma retail is most effective when it is aligned with the pharmacy's fundamental role: safe access to medicines, continuity of care, and community health support. Unlike conventional retail, pharmacy marketing cannot rely on urgency, emotional manipulation, or excessive promotion. It must be built on credibility, ethical communication, and service reliability.

Local marketing tools, pamphlets, WhatsApp communication, and community engagement, remain highly effective when they prioritise utility and trust. Digital channels strengthen discoverability and legitimacy, particularly through Google Business Profile optimisation and consistent educational content. Professional collaboration through doctor connects and health camps integrates the pharmacy into the local healthcare ecosystem and strengthens patient continuity. Loyalty programs succeed when they reduce friction, reinforce habit, and reward long-term engagement rather than promoting indiscriminate consumption.

Ultimately, the strongest marketing strategy for a pharmacy is not a campaign. It is a system. A pharmacy that is operationally disciplined, patient-friendly, ethically consistent, and community-present will create marketing momentum that is difficult for competitors to replicate. Marketing then becomes not a loud overlay on the business, but a natural outcome of a well-run healthcare retail institution.

References

- https://www.marketingweek.com/boots-growing-sales-focus-on-value/
- https://www.marketingweek.com/boots-christmas-personal-2024/
- https://www.campaignlive.co.uk/article/campaign-tech-awards-winners-2024-best-use-data-retail/1874107
- https://www.boots-uk.com/media/1hii4dxm/wba_esg-impact-report-24.pdf
- https://www.pharmacymagazine.co.uk/retailer-news/boots-posts-12th-quarter-of-retail-market-share-growth
- https://www.who.int/publications/i/item/WHO-TRS-961
- https://www.fip.org/good_pharmacy_practice
- https://www.who.int/initiatives/medication-without-harm

Chapter 11

E-commerce & Omnichannel Strategy

E-commerce is no longer an add-on for pharmacy businesses but a strategic capability. Even traditional brick-and-mortar pharmacies now compete in a world where customers expect to start a health journey on their phones, continue it in a store, and have follow-up delivered to their doorstep. The winning pharmacies will be those that design seamless experiences spanning digital and physical touchpoints, while meeting the unique safety, legal, and logistical challenges of medicines. This chapter explains how to build an omnichannel pharmacy strategy: how to integrate stores and digital, handle online orders and e-prescriptions safely, design logistics (including cold-chain), select partnership models with marketplaces, and choose a technology stack (apps, chatbots, and analytics) that delivers measurable business and clinical value.

Why Omnichannel Matters in Pharmacy

Omnichannel is about more than adding a website or an app. It is about creating continuity of experience across every customer touchpoint. For pharmacies, the stakes are higher than for most retail categories because the product is healthcare. Continuity of care, medicine safety, regulatory compliance, and patient trust become part of the omnichannel brief. Key drivers that make omnichannel essential today:

- **Customer expectation:** Consumers expect choice, click-to-collect, home delivery, scheduled refills, and teleconsult integration. The pandemic accelerated these expectations, and they have become sticky. Evidence from market research shows significant and accelerating growth in e-pharmacy adoption.

- **Retention through convenience:** Omnichannel reduces friction at renewal points (refill reminders, e-prescriptions), increasing adherence and repeat purchases, both commercially valuable and clinically important.
- **Data advantage:** Integrated channels generate richer customer signals (purchase history + in-store interactions + digital behaviour), enabling better personalization, inventory planning, and risk management.
- **Competitive defense:** Large marketplace players and digitally native startups are aggressive in pricing and logistics. For traditional pharmacy groups, omnichannel is both offense and defense: it prevents customer churn and enables platform partnerships.

Omnichannel success requires a clear industry mindset shift: treat the pharmacy as a care platform rather than a single point of sale. That means connecting clinical workflows (prescriptions, counselling) and retail workflows (inventory, billing, loyalty) across channels.

Omnichannel Design Principles for Pharmacies

Designing an omnichannel pharmacy requires business rules and UX rules that respect safety and make the customer journey effortless. The following principles should guide every decision:

- **Single source of truth (inventory & patient record).** The same inventory, pricing, and relevant patient information must be visible across store systems and digital channels to prevent stock-outs, inconsistent pricing, or unsafe substitutions. Real-time integration is essential for medicines.
- **Clinical gating.** Clinical checkpoints—pharmacist review, Schedule H/X validation, allergy checks—should not

be bypassable by the digital flow. An online order is not complete until clinically cleared. This preserves safety and regulatory compliance.

- **Seamless handoffs.** A customer must be able to begin an action in one channel (search, prescription upload) and complete it in another (pickup, pharmacist counselling) without re-entering information. Handoffs should be smooth and secure.
- **Flexible fulfilment.** Offer multiple fulfilment options, same-day delivery, scheduled delivery, ship-from-store, click-and-collect, and ensure the inventory engine routes orders optimally by cost, speed, and compliance.
- **Transparent communication.** Customers must always be told where their order is, what substitution rules are applied, and when to expect delivery. Transparency reduces queries and trust erosion.
- **Regulatory first.** Every digital feature must be assessed against local drug laws (e-prescription acceptance, controlled substances, telemedicine integration). When in doubt, default to the stricter interpretation. In India, regulators have been active in policing online sales of prescription medicines, underlining the importance of compliance.

Typical Omnichannel Customer Journeys

Map common journeys and define SOPs for each. Examples:

1. **Refill (digital → delivery):**
    - Customer receives automated refill reminder.
    - Uploads the previous prescription or uses the stored e-prescription.

- Pharmacist validates and authorizes; order is routed to the nearest store for dispatch or to a central warehouse for ship-from-hub fulfilment.
- Customer receives delivery with pharmacist contact for counselling.

2. **Acute purchase (mobile search → click & collect):**
   - Customer searches on the app, finds product, and selects same-day click & collect.
   - Store reserves item, notifies customer, pharmacist prepares the packet.
   - The customer picks up and receives a brief counselling or printed drug information.

3. **Teleconsult + e-prescription (telemedicine integrated):**
   - Patient has a teleconsult with a clinician (internal or partner).
   - Clinician issues an e-prescription forwarded to the pharmacy platform.
   - Pharmacist verifies and dispenses; if controlled medicine is involved, compliance workflows kick in (document logging, verification).

4. **Marketplace referral → pharmacist review → home delivery:**
   - Customer buys via a marketplace (platform acts as lead).
   - Marketplace routes orders to a network pharmacy that validates prescriptions before fulfillment.
   - A pharmacist may request a clearer prescription photo or call the patient; fulfillment follows compliance SOPs.

For each journey, document who performs which task, what checks are required, where data is stored, and how exceptions are handled.

Handling Online Orders: Operational Flows & Policies

Online ordering magnifies operational complexity. Successful operators treat it as a separate but integrated stream with dedicated SOPs for volume, exceptions, and compliance.

Order Intake & Triage

- **Automated validation:** On order receipt, the system should perform automated checks: prescription presence (if required), product age limits, OTC vs prescription classification, and basic fraud flags.
- **Clinical triage:** Orders that the system flags—incomplete prescriptions, Schedule H/X items, or high-value/controlled orders—should be routed to a pharmacist queue for manual review.
- **Acknowledgement & SLA promise:** Immediately acknowledge the order and provide a realistic SLA (e.g., "Same day if ordered before 2 pm" or "48–72 hours"). Under-promise and over-deliver to build trust.

Substitutions & Inventory Shortfall

- **Pre-approved substitutions:** Enable customers to set preferences for substitutions (no substitution / only generic / pharmacist may substitute up to X% cheaper). Default should be conservative—require affirmative consent for substitution on prescription medicines.
- **Reserve inventory:** For drugs under prescription that are critical (chronics), systems can auto-reserve for repeat customers to minimise disruptions.

- **Out-of-stock escalation:** Automated alerts to procurement teams with recommended substitutes and reorder suggestions based on lead time.

Payment and Fraud Controls

- **Payment options:** Cash on delivery (COD) remains popular in many markets, but digital payments reduce reconciliation friction. For regulated medicines, many operators restrict COD or require pre-payment to reduce fraud.
- **Fraud detection:** Validate new accounts, flag suspicious bulk orders, and implement velocity checks (too many orders in a short time). High-risk orders require pharmacist or manager approval.

Order Fulfilment & Chain of Custody

- **Pick & pack SOPs:** Items must be picked from designated areas, checked against the order by barcode scan, and packed in tamper-evident packaging when needed. For cold-chain items, use validated insulated packaging with temperature indicators.
- **Dispatch & tracking:** Provide real-time tracking and maintain chain-of-custody records (time, person, store). These logs are invaluable for audits and incident resolution.
- **Delivery signature & verification:** For controlled drugs or expensive biologics, require recipient verification and signature; capture identity data where local laws permit.

Returns & Adverse Events

- **Clear returns policy:** Define what can be returned—unopened OTCs, damaged items, and what cannot (dispensed prescription medicines generally should not be accepted back for resale).

- **Adverse event reporting:** Create SOPs for handling adverse event reports from online customers, including immediate pharmacist escalation and regulatory reporting if required.

Operational robustness is built from SOPs that convert digital orders into predictable in-store actions and that retain traceability throughout the lifecycle.

E-Prescriptions: Legality, Acceptance & Verification

E-prescriptions are central to digital pharmacy workflows, but acceptance varies by jurisdiction. There are three pragmatic steps for any omnichannel pharmacy:

1. **Understand local legal status:** Confirm whether e-prescriptions are legally valid, which formats are accepted (scans, structured e-prescriptions), and how Schedule H/H1/X medicines must be handled. In many countries, regulators have actively clarified online pharmacy responsibilities; in India, for example, authorities have scrutinised online sales and the handling of prescription drugs—operators must ensure compliance with CDSCO rules.
2. **Implement secure submission & storage:** E-prescriptions must be uploaded and stored securely, with clear audit trails (who uploaded, who verified, time stamps). Use encrypted storage and role-based access controls. Retention periods should meet statutory requirements.
3. **Verification & pharmacist review:** Even when a prescription looks correct, a pharmacist must verify prescriber identity (where possible), check for obvious interactions/allergies, and confirm dosing. For higher-risk

medicines, a telephone confirmation with the prescriber or patient may be appropriate.

Operational tip: offer templated clinician integrations (APIs to telemedicine partners) to receive structured e-prescriptions; this reduces transcription errors compared to scanned images.

Logistics: Last-Mile, Cold Chain & Sustainability

Logistics is the linchpin of e-pharmacy. Delivery models must balance speed, cost, and medicine safety.

Fulfilment Models

- **Ship from Store (SFS):** Stores act as micro-fulfilment centres. SFS reduces delivery time and costs for neighbourhood orders and uses existing inventory. It suits chains with dense store networks.
- **Centralised fulfilment (hub & spoke):** A central warehouse handles stock for non-urgent and high-volume SKUs, enabling tighter inventory control and cost efficiency. Best for curated assortments and longer-lead items.
- **Hybrid:** Use SFS for fast movers and critical medicines; use central warehouses for less time-sensitive items and consumables.

Choice depends on store density, SKU characteristics, and expected SLAs.

Cold Chain for Temperature-Sensitive Meds

Vaccines, insulin, biologics, and certain injectables require temperature control. Cold-chain is non-negotiable and must be validated end-to-end.

Key elements:

- **Equipment & qualification:** Use WHO-recommended or GDP-compliant refrigerators, validated insulated packaging, and temperature monitoring devices. Regularly calibrate and qualify equipment.
- **Monitoring & alerts:** IoT temperature sensors with alerts help catch excursions early. Maintain temperature logs and corrective action records.
- **Transport packaging:** Insulated shippers with qualified phase-change materials and temperature loggers ensure product integrity during transport.
- **Training & SOPs:** Drivers and pickers must know cold-chain SOPs: pack time limits, maximum exposure times, and what to do in an excursion.

Cold-chain failures are reputational and clinical risks, particularly for vaccines and insulin, and must be managed with the same rigour as clinical protocols.

Last-Mile Considerations

- **Route optimisation:** Use routing algorithms to batch deliveries for efficiency while meeting SLA promises.
- **Delivery professionalism:** Drivers should be trained in handling fragile and sensitive medical packages and in customer verification protocols.
- **Contactless & timed delivery:** Offer time windows and contactless options; these improve customer satisfaction and decrease failed delivery attempts.

Sustainability & Reverse Logistics

- **Eco-packing:** Use recyclable insulation and optimise package sizing to reduce waste.

- **Reverse logistics:** Define safe disposal and return processes—for example, expired or recalled items—ensuring regulatory compliance and traceability.

Partnership Models With Online Marketplaces & Telemedicine

Marketplace partnerships accelerate reach but introduce complexity in control, compliance, and margin sharing. Typical models:

1. **Lead/referral model:** Marketplace generates demand and refers customers to licensed pharmacies. Fulfilment and pharmacist accountability remain with the pharmacy. This model provides demand without losing operational control; legal accountability still rests with the dispensing pharmacy. Regulators often scrutinise marketplace roles in medicine sale pathways.
2. **Marketplace as fulfilment platform:** Marketplace aggregates orders and assigns fulfilment to partner pharmacies. This provides scale but requires robust SLAs and integration for prescription validation.
3. **White-label/plug-in:** Pharmacy's systems are embedded in marketplace UI (via APIs), giving customers native checkout but maintaining pharmacy control over dispensing and logistics.
4. **Strategic alliances with telemedicine:** Deeper clinical integration—where teleconsults are bundled with pharmacy fulfilment—can create one-stop care journeys. Ensuring clinical governance and clear boundaries between prescribers and dispensers is essential.

When selecting partners, evaluate:

- Regulatory posture of the platform.
- Data privacy and ownership.
- Financial terms and customer ownership.
- Operational SLAs on prescription validation and delivery.

Technology Stack: Essential Components

A practical omnichannel tech stack is modular, secure, and tightly integrated. Core layers:

- **Customer frontends:** Mobile app + responsive website + marketplace connectors. Provide unified profiles, order history, and refill reminders.
- **Order management system (OMS):** Central orchestrator that receives orders from frontends and marketplaces, applies rules (prescription needed, substitution policies), and routes fulfilment.
- **Inventory & POS integration:** Real-time inventory sync between stores, warehouses, and online channels. POS systems should update OMS in seconds to avoid overselling.
- **Pharmacist clinical module:** A review dashboard for pharmacists with prescription viewer, interaction checks, allergy flags and counselling notes. This is the clinical heart of the stack.
- **Logistics & WMS:** Warehouse Management System for hubs and routing tools for last-mile. Integrate temperature monitoring for cold chain.
- **Payments & fraud:** Secure payment gateway integration and anti-fraud tools.
- **Customer engagement layer:** Messaging, push notifications, email, and chatbot integration.
- **Analytics & BI:** Dashboards for inventory turnover, fulfilment KPIs, customer cohorts, and clinical safety metrics. Advanced analytics supports propensity-to-refill models and personalization.
- **Security & compliance:** Encryption, IAM (identity & access management), audit trails, and data retention modules as per law.

Modern architectures favour API-first, event-driven systems so components can be upgraded without rewriting the entire platform.

Apps, Chatbots & Conversational Commerce

Digital frontends are where customers interact; they must be fast, clear and clinically safe.

Mobile apps: must-have features

- Prescription upload (photo + structured e-prescription support)
- Refill scheduler and reminders
- Order tracking and delivery schedule
- Secure messaging with pharmacist
- Wallet / subscription plans (for chronic therapies)
- Educational content and medicine information

Apps should reduce friction for routine tasks (refills) and make high-touch actions easy (contact pharmacist).

Chatbots: Scope and Safe Design

Chatbots can automate intake (order status, basic FAQs) and triage simple clinical queries, but they must be carefully scoped:

- **Transactional chatbots** can handle order lookups, payment troubles and fulfilment queries safely.
- **Clinical chatbots** that provide medicine advice are high risk. If used, they must be conservative (provide general information only), clearly label themselves as non-clinical, and escalate to pharmacists for any therapy-related questions. Research suggests chatbots can improve adherence and education but must be designed with privacy, accuracy and escalation pathways in mind.

Always log conversations and provide a clear path to human escalation.

Analytics, KPIs & Measurement

Analytics turns omnichannel activity into continuous improvement. Key KPI clusters:

- **Customer metrics:** Active customers, retention, repeat rate, lifetime value, net promoter score (NPS).
- **Fulfilment metrics:** On-time delivery %, order cycle time, first-attempt delivery, order accuracy.
- **Inventory metrics:** Days of inventory (DOI), stock-out rate for critical SKUs, shrinkage, and expiry rate.
- **Clinical safety metrics:** Prescription rejection rate (due to errors), adverse event reports, and counselling compliance rate.
- **Operational efficiency:** Picks per hour, driver utilisation, average basket size, cost per order.

Advanced analytics use machine learning to predict refill likelihood, identify at-risk adherence cohorts, and optimise safety checks based on patient-level risk.

People, Process & Governance

Technology is only an enabler. People and processes make omnichannel safe and reliable.

- **Roles & responsibilities:** Define clear ownership for online orders, pharmacist clinical review, logistics exceptions, and marketplace disputes.
- **Training & SOPs:** Train staff on new digital SOPs (e-prescription handling, click & collect, cold chain packing). Conduct periodic audits and scenario drills.

- **Regulatory governance:** Maintain a compliance register, audit logs, and a designated compliance officer responsible for marketplace relationships and digital policies.
- **Incident management:** Incident response playbooks for delivery failures, cold-chain excursions, or adverse event reports. Capture root cause and corrective actions.

Good governance balances speed with clinical safeguards.

Risk, Privacy & Data Protection

Digital channels amplify privacy obligations. Pharmacies must treat health data with the highest care.

- **Data minimisation:** Store only what's necessary; encrypt data at rest and in transit.
- **Consent & transparency:** Obtain clear consent for e-prescription use, messaging, and data sharing with partners (marketplaces, telemedicine providers).
- **Third-party risk:** Vendors and marketplaces must meet security standards. Conduct vendor due diligence and include data protection clauses.
- **Local law & cross-border flow:** Be aware of cross-border considerations for data and cloud hosting; follow local rules on health data residency if applicable.

A data breach in a healthcare context can be materially harmful to patients and the business.

Commercial Models & Pricing in Omnichannel

Omnichannel economics differs from pure retail. Consider:

- **Fulfilment cost layering:** Ship-from-store can be cheaper for nearby orders; hub fulfilment is more efficient for bulk items. Model margins per channel.

- **Subscription & health plans:** Chronic patients respond well to subscription models (monthly refills with discounted pricing and auto-fulfilment). These stabilize demand and improve retention.
- **Marketplace economics:** Referral fees and diluted customer ownership are tradeoffs for reach. Negotiate for customer contact data and co-branded experiences where possible.
- **Promotions & price parity:** Maintain pricing consistency across channels or communicate differences transparently; avoid eroding margins with unplanned discounts on marketplaces.

Implementation Roadmap (Practical Checklist)

A phased rollout reduces risk:

1. **Proof of concept (3 months):** Launch a minimal app/website for a small customer cohort; validate refill workflows and basic delivery.
2. **Operational pilot (3–6 months):** Expand to a handful of stores; test ship-from-store, cold-chain packing, and pharmacist review dashboards.
3. **Marketplace integration (6–9 months):** Connect to one marketplace with clear SLAs and compliance integration.
4. **Scale & analytics (9–18 months):** Roll out across network, implement advanced analytics, loyalty programs, and telemedicine integrations.

Accompany each phase with training, SOP updates, and compliance reviews.

Case Highlights & Practical Lessons

- Reservation beats apology. Reserve critical chronic medicines for subscription customers; reduce stock-out churn.

- Clinical review is non-negotiable. Fast fulfilment must not bypass pharmacist sign-off for prescriptions.
- Measure everything. Track cancelled orders, time to pharmacist review, temperature excursions, and returns; fix the fastest-moving bottlenecks first.
- Partner selectively. Marketplaces drive volume but require contractual clarity about compliance and customer data.
- Start small with the cold chain. Validate packaging and monitoring at pilot scale before scaling expensive cold-chain fulfilment.

Omnichannel strategy in pharmacy is a business transformation, not merely a technology project. It blends retail discipline with clinical governance and logistic precision. Successful operators treat digital channels as extensions of clinical care—designing flows where safety, clarity, and convenience are embedded by design.

The technology choices—a resilient OMS, real-time inventory sync, secure e-prescription handling, and intelligent routing—are important. But even more important are the SOPs that map digital orders into reliable in-store actions and the governance that keeps clinical safeguards intact.

Pharmacies that master omnichannel will deliver better health outcomes for patients, higher retention for the business, and resilience in a marketplace that increasingly values convenience delivered safely. With careful design, disciplined execution and responsible partnerships, omnichannel becomes not just a competitive advantage but a new standard for responsible pharmacy care.

References

- India online pharmacy market overview (IMARC Group). (IMARC Group)
- https://www.imarcgroup.com/india-online-pharmacy-market

- Regulation of e-pharmacies in India (analysis & case notes). (SRL)
- https://spiceroutelegal.com/publications/regulation-of-e-pharmacies-in-india/
- CDSCO—Digital Drugs Regulatory System (DDRS) and related documents (Govt. of India). (CDSCO)
- https://cdsco.gov.in/opencms/export/sites/CDSCO_WEB/Pdf-documents/EoI_DDRS_CDSCO_2ndnov23.pdf
- WHO immunization and cold-chain guidance (vaccine storage and logistics). (World Health Organization)
- https://cdn.who.int/media/docs/default-source/searo/india/publications/immunization-handbook-107-198-part2.pdf
- TechMagnate: Online Pharmacy Trends India FY'24 (market search analysis). (Techmagnate)
- https://www.techmagnate.com/wp-content/uploads/2024/05/Online-Pharmacy-Trends-India-FY_24new.pdf
- MedCityNews: The omnichannel strategy of retail health (industry commentary). (MedCity News)
- https://medcitynews.com/2022/09/the-omnichannel-strategy-of-retail-health/
- Cold chain and logistics trends & best practices (industry overview).
- https://www.tempcontrolpack.com/knowledge/pharma-cold-chain-logistics-safe-delivery-in-2025/
- https://shipsy.io/blogs/cold-chain-logistics-ensuring-safe/
- Chatbots in pharmacy—potential and limitations (review).
- Market research: India E-Pharmacy & Telemedicine forecasts. (Ken Research)
- https://www.kenresearch.com/india-e-pharmacy-and-telemedicine-market

Chapter 12

Expanding the Chain

Expansion is the moment when a pharmacy business moves from intent to consequence. Opening a second store feels like growth. Opening the tenth changes the nature of the business entirely. Expanding a pharmacy chain is not simply about adding locations. It is about replicating trust, discipline, and quality across geographies while managing complexity that increases faster than revenue.

Many pharmacy businesses underestimate what expansion truly demands. Early success often creates confidence that past methods will scale naturally. In reality, growth exposes every weakness in operations, governance, people systems, and decision-making. Processes that worked under close owner supervision begin to fray. Cultural cues weaken. Inconsistencies creep in quietly, long before they show up in financial statements or regulatory notices.

Pharmacy expansion carries unique responsibility. Unlike fashion or food retail, the product is health. Errors are not confined to customer dissatisfaction or margin erosion. They affect patient safety, regulatory standing, and professional credibility. Expansion therefore must be intentional, data-informed, and operationally grounded.

This chapter examines what it takes to expand a pharmacy chain responsibly and sustainably. It focuses on market research for new locations, franchising models and best practices, maintaining brand uniformity and service quality at scale, and the real challenges faced by fast-scaling pharmacy chains. The emphasis throughout is on building repeatable excellence rather than chasing rapid footprint growth.

Understanding Expansion as a System, Not a Project

Expansion should be treated as a system-level transformation, not a series of isolated store launches. Each new location adds complexity across supply chain, staffing, compliance, technology, and customer experience. Without a systems mindset, expansion magnifies inefficiencies and exposes the organization to risk.

Successful chains understand that scale changes the role of leadership. Founders and senior managers must move from direct supervision to system design. Decisions shift from intuition to data. Control shifts from presence to process. This transition is uncomfortable but necessary.

Expansion also changes internal expectations. Store teams look to central leadership for clarity. Vendors expect consistency. Regulators expect maturity. Customers expect the same experience everywhere. A growing chain must therefore behave like an institution, not a collection of independent outlets.

Market Research as the Foundation of Expansion

Market research is the first discipline that separates thoughtful expansion from speculative growth. Opening new stores based on anecdotal demand, competitor presence, or emotional attachment to locations leads to uneven performance and capital strain. Effective market research begins with understanding demand drivers specific to pharmacy retail. Population density alone is insufficient. Demographics matter deeply. Areas with higher prevalence of chronic diseases, older populations, or dense residential clusters generate different demand patterns compared to transient commercial zones.

Prescription intensity is a critical indicator. Locations near hospitals, diagnostic centers, clinics, and nursing homes tend to generate sustained prescription traffic. However, proximity alone is not enough. The quality and type of medical practice in the area influence prescription volumes, medicine mix, and price sensitivity.

Competition analysis must go beyond counting nearby pharmacies. It should examine their positioning, operating hours, service quality, stock depth, and pricing discipline. A market crowded with poorly run pharmacies may still represent opportunity. A market dominated by a trusted local player may require a differentiated strategy. Footfall patterns deserve careful study. Pharmacies benefit from habitual visits rather than impulse traffic. Residential catchments, daily commute paths, and access convenience matter more than premium retail frontage. Parking availability, walkability, and visibility from common paths all influence repeat visits.

Economic factors must be assessed realistically. Income levels affect brand preferences, generic acceptance, and willingness to pay for convenience services such as home delivery or subscriptions. Overestimating purchasing power leads to inventory mismatches and slow-moving stock. Regulatory environment varies across regions and must be factored in. Local enforcement intensity, inspector behavior, and licensing timelines can significantly affect store viability. Expansion plans that ignore regulatory realities often face costly delays.

The most disciplined chains formalize market research into a scoring model. Locations are evaluated against weighted criteria covering demand, competition, cost structure, compliance risk, and long-term growth potential. This reduces emotional decision-making and creates accountability for expansion outcomes.

Site Selection and Store Economics

Once a market is shortlisted, site selection determines commercial viability. Rent is often the single largest fixed cost in pharmacy retail, and poor rent decisions undermine even strong sales. The temptation to secure high-visibility sites must be balanced against sustainable economics. Pharmacies do not benefit from impulse browsing in the same way as lifestyle retail. Accessibility and convenience outweigh prestige locations.

Store size must be right-sized. Oversized stores increase rental burden and operational complexity without proportionate revenue upside. Undersized stores struggle with inventory organization, counselling space, and staff efficiency. Optimal sizing supports workflow clarity and compliance.

Store economics should be modeled conservatively. Break-even timelines must account for slower ramp-up in new markets. Initial prescription flow builds gradually as trust forms. Aggressive revenue assumptions create pressure that leads to shortcuts. Capital expenditure must include more than interiors and fixtures. Technology setup, initial inventory, staff training, licensing costs, and working capital buffers are essential components. Under-capitalized expansion leads to operational fragility.

Franchising as an Expansion Model

Franchising offers a path to faster expansion with lower capital deployment, but it introduces its own complexity. In pharmacy retail, franchising must be approached cautiously due to regulatory, ethical, and quality considerations.

At its best, franchising allows local entrepreneurship to combine with centralized systems and brand strength. Franchise partners bring local market knowledge, capital, and day-to-day management commitment. The brand provides SOPs, procurement leverage, training, and technology. However, franchising in pharmacy is fundamentally different from food or apparel. Compliance cannot be delegated loosely. The brand remains exposed to regulatory and reputational risk arising from franchisee behavior.

Successful pharmacy franchising begins with rigorous partner selection. Financial capacity alone is insufficient. Franchisees must demonstrate professional seriousness, compliance orientation, and willingness to follow standardized processes. Cultural alignment matters more than expansion speed. Clear role definition is critical. Clinical responsibilities, pharmacist employment, documentation standards, and audit rights must be unambiguous. Ambiguity becomes conflict during inspections or adverse events.

Franchise agreements must prioritize quality and compliance over revenue extraction. Excessive franchise fees or unrealistic sales targets push partners toward shortcuts. Sustainable franchising aligns incentives around long-term trust and stability.

Training is the backbone of franchising. Initial onboarding must be comprehensive, covering not only operations but also brand philosophy, ethical standards, and regulatory expectations. Ongoing training reinforces consistency and adapts partners to evolving standards.

Audit mechanisms must be robust and routine. Surprise audits, mystery shopping, and performance scorecards help maintain discipline. The goal is not punishment but early correction. Franchising works best when the brand has already proven replicability through company-owned stores. Using franchising to discover operational weaknesses is risky. Systems should be mature before being multiplied.

Maintaining Brand Uniformity Across Locations

Brand uniformity is not about identical interiors or identical promotions. It is about consistent experience, behavior, and trust signals. Customers should feel they are in the same pharmacy chain regardless of location. Uniformity begins with visual standards. Store layout, signage, staff uniforms, and display norms should follow clear guidelines. Visual chaos signals operational chaos. Order communicates professionalism.

Service standards are even more important. Greeting protocols, counselling quality, billing transparency, and complaint handling must be consistent. Variability in service erodes brand credibility faster than pricing differences. Inventory standards play a key role. Core assortments must be available everywhere. Customers expect continuity, especially for chronic medicines. Local customization should exist at the margin, not at the core.

Technology is a powerful enabler of uniformity. Centralized POS systems, inventory management, and CRM platforms reduce deviation. Data visibility allows central teams to identify anomalies early. Communication discipline supports uniformity. Changes in pricing, promotions, SOPs, or regulatory guidelines must be communicated clearly and implemented uniformly. Partial adoption creates confusion and resentment.

Leadership behavior sets the tone. When central teams enforce standards selectively, inconsistency becomes cultural. Uniformity must be non-negotiable at the core while allowing controlled flexibility at the edges.

Protecting Service Quality at Scale

Service quality is often the first casualty of rapid expansion. New stores are staffed quickly, trained unevenly, and placed under revenue pressure. Without safeguards, the customer experience degrades silently. Pharmacy service quality depends heavily on people. Pharmacists and support staff must be trained not just in tasks but in judgment. Expansion strategies must therefore include talent pipelines.

Hiring standards should not be diluted to meet timelines. It is better to delay a store opening than to operate with underqualified or untrained staff. Regulatory consequences of poor staffing are severe. Training programs must evolve with scale. Informal shadowing works in small teams but fails across multiple locations. Structured training modules, assessments, and certifications create consistency. Performance measurement must include quality indicators, not just sales. Counselling compliance, documentation accuracy, complaint resolution time, and audit scores should influence evaluations.

Workload management matters. Overburdened staff cut corners. Staffing models must reflect realistic footfall and prescription volumes. Cost control achieved by understaffing leads to long-term damage. Service culture must be reinforced continually. Recognition, feedback, and visible leadership engagement reinforce expectations. Culture does not scale automatically. It must be cultivated intentionally.

Operational Challenges in Fast-Scaling Chains

Fast-scaling pharmacy chains face predictable challenges. Inventory imbalances increase as demand forecasting struggles to keep up with geographic diversity. Stock-outs coexist with dead stock.

Supply chain strain emerges. Vendors struggle to meet expanded demand. Credit terms tighten. Logistics complexity grows, particularly for temperature-sensitive products.

Compliance risk multiplies. Each additional store increases inspection exposure. Inconsistent documentation practices become harder to monitor. One non-compliant store can attract scrutiny across the chain. Technology strain is common. Systems built for a handful of stores struggle at scale. Performance issues, data inconsistencies, and integration gaps surface under load.

Cultural dilution occurs. Early employees who embodied the brand values are outnumbered by new hires who lack context. Informal norms weaken. Behavior becomes transactional. Leadership bandwidth becomes a constraint. Founders and senior leaders cannot personally oversee everything. Without middle management depth, decision quality suffers. These challenges are not signs of failure.

They are predictable consequences of growth. The difference between resilient and fragile chains lies in how early these challenges are anticipated and addressed.

Lessons from Fast-Scaling Pharmacy Chains

Experience across markets shows recurring lessons. First, speed without stability is dangerous. Opening many stores quickly without operational readiness leads to cascading failures that are expensive to fix. Next, systems must precede scale. SOPs, training, audits, and technology should be robust before aggressive expansion begins. Moreover, compliance must be embedded, not enforced. Cultures built on fear of inspection eventually crack. Cultures built on professional pride endure. Besides, local adaptation must be controlled. Total standardization ignores market realities. Excessive flexibility destroys brand integrity. Successful chains define clear boundaries. On top of that, people strategy determines outcome. Investment in leadership development, pharmacist engagement, and staff retention pays dividends over time. Aditionally, expansion should be reversible. Lease terms, inventory commitments, and capital allocation should allow correction if a location underperforms. Irreversible decisions amplify risk.

Building a Sustainable Expansion Roadmap

A disciplined expansion roadmap balances ambition with capacity. Phased growth allows learning to compound. Pilot clusters enable operational refinement before replication. Metrics must guide decisions. Store-level profitability, compliance scores, customer retention, and staff stability provide early warning signals. Growth should pause if fundamentals weaken.

Capital allocation must remain conservative. Expansion should not starve existing stores of attention or resources. Strong cores support healthy growth. Governance structures must mature. Clear escalation paths, audit cycles, and decision rights reduce confusion. Transparency builds internal trust.

Most importantly, expansion must remain aligned with purpose. Pharmacy chains exist to serve health needs responsibly. Growth that compromises safety or ethics undermines long-term value. Expanding a pharmacy chain is one of the most demanding phases in the life of the business. It tests discipline, patience, and leadership maturity. The excitement of growth must be balanced by respect for complexity and responsibility. Successful expansion is not measured by store count alone. It is measured by consistency of care, resilience of operations, and durability of trust. Chains that grow thoughtfully build institutions. Chains that grow recklessly build risk.

Market research grounds expansion in reality. Franchising, when done responsibly, enables partnership-driven growth. Uniform standards protect brand credibility. Service quality sustains loyalty. Lessons from fast-scaling chains remind leaders that systems matter more than speed.

In a sector where trust is everything, expansion done right strengthens the brand and broadens access to care. Expansion done poorly weakens both. The difference lies in discipline, foresight, and respect for the unique responsibility that pharmacy retail carries.

References

- https://cdsco.gov.in/opencms/opencms/en/Home/
- https://cdsco.gov.in/opencms/opencms/en/Acts-Rules/
- https://pharmacycouncil.nic.in/
- https://www.who.int/publications/i/item/WHO-TRS-961
- https://www.fip.org/good_pharmacy_practice
- https://www.imarcgroup.com/india-pharmacy-retail-market
- https://www.kenresearch.com/india-retail-pharmacy-market

- https://www.mckinsey.com/industries/healthcare/our-insights
- https://hbr.org/topic/growth-strategy
- https://www2.deloitte.com/global/en/industries/life-sciences-and-healthcare.html

Chapter 13

Seasonal and Emergency Demand Management

Framing demand as a predictable inflow of customers does not capture the reality of pharmacy retail. Demand in this industry is shaped by health itself: sickness, uncertainty, public advisories, weather changes, and epidemics influence how people seek care and medicines. During normal periods, pharmacies are judged on convenience, reliability, friendliness, and pricing. During demand surges, the stakes are higher. Availability becomes a matter of trust. Clarity becomes a necessity. Fairness becomes a moral imperative.

Seasonal and emergency demand management is one of the most demanding and revealing functions in pharmacy operations. It involves systems, people, and judgment. It is an arena where operational readiness meets invisible human needs. How a pharmacy chain navigates demand spikes sends a clear message to the community about its capability and character. A thoughtful response builds trust that lasts. A mismanaged response undermines confidence that took years to build.

In this chapter, we will examine three interconnected dimensions of demand management. First, how to manage spikes that arise during recurring seasonal illnesses or localized health crises. Second, the discipline required to prepare for and coordinate vaccine supply and operations during pandemics. Third, how to design and execute stocking strategies that address sudden surges in demand without compromising fairness, ethics, or long-term viability.

Each dimension requires unique approaches but is held together by common principles: foresight, clarity, discipline, and humanity.

Managing Spikes During Flu Season or Health Crises

Seasonal demand patterns represent some of the earliest challenges for pharmacy operations. Flu seasons arrive reliably every year, yet their manifestation is not uniform or simple. Some years present early, sharp spikes. Others unfold slowly with multiple peaks. In tropical climates, respiratory illnesses may coincide with monsoon changeovers, pollution peaks, or humidity fluctuations. Successful pharmacy chains do not treat seasonal spikes as afterthoughts. They treat them as recurring strategic events that require preparation, coordination, and reflection.

The impact of seasonal spikes is often most visible in specific product categories. Antipyretics and analgesics become common purchases. Cough syrups and lozenges see increased movement. Inhalers and respiratory support products rise in demand. Diagnostic tools such as thermometers and rapid fever test kits move off shelves quickly. However, secondary demand flows also emerge. Short courses of antibiotics are sought, sometimes inappropriately, driven by public fear rather than clinical necessity. Pharmacies must therefore manage not only the operational flow of products but also the clinical appropriateness of dispensing.

The first step in managing seasonal spikes is understanding patterns, not assumptions. Historical sales data is valuable, but it must be examined with nuance. A single year's trend is insufficient. Multi-year analysis identifies outliers, shifts in timing, and region-specific behaviors. Surrounding conditions matter. A cold wave in one region might precede a spike by several weeks. Air quality issues in another city might drive respiratory product demand ahead of typical flu seasons. Compartmentalising seasons into fixed months misses important local dynamics.

Staff preparation is as important as inventory. Seasonal demand does not just increase customer numbers: It increases interaction intensity. People in pain or worry ask more questions. They need reassurance as much as they need medicine. Pharmacy teams must respond with patience, empathy, and clarity. This means adjusting staffing rosters, balancing clinical and support roles, and planning breaks to avoid fatigue. Without attention to workforce readiness, accuracy and compliance commonly deteriorate under sustained pressure.

Operational practices must be reinforced, not loosened, during spikes. Standing orders, prescription checks, documentation, and patient counselling remain critical. In fact, the chaos of high footfall increases the risk of error if discipline slips. Transaction speed cannot be elevated at the cost of clinical safety.

During localized health crises such as dengue outbreaks, viral fever clusters, or waterborne illness spikes, demand may escalate abruptly. In these moments, community needs can outpace routine planning. Pharmacies become touchpoints for information as well as supply. Customers come not just for medicines but for clarity on symptoms, combination therapies, and next steps. Staff training should include communication protocols for common concerns. Teams need guidance on what to say, what to defer to clinicians, and how to refer customers respectfully to healthcare professionals when appropriate.

Communication discipline is a critical tool. In an age of rapid social media spread, misinformation circulates easily. Pharmacy teams must avoid speculation and stick to factual, consistent messages. A calm, transparent explanation of availability, timelines, and safe usage reinforces public confidence.

Ethical judgment becomes central. Hoarding behavior tends to emerge quickly as fear spreads. Customers attempt bulk purchases for family stores or anticipated shortages. Pharmacy chains must introduce and enforce sensible quantity limits for critical products. Such limits protect broader access without creating panic. They should be applied uniformly and explained with empathy. A consistent policy across stores reduces confusion and conflict.

Coordination with local healthcare providers can enhance responsiveness. Informal communication with neighborhood clinics, diagnostic centers, and hospitals often provides early signals of rising caseloads. These signals may arrive ahead of formal public health announcements or sales spikes. Pharmacy chains that build collaborative relationships with local practitioners gain informal intelligence that informs inventory and staffing decisions.

Crucially, seasonal demand should be analysed thoughtfully after the fact. Each flu season or health spike reveals insights about customer behavior, supply gaps, staffing pressure points, and communication bottlenecks. Post-season review sessions involving cross-functional teams help identify what worked, what did not, and what should change. This reflective discipline transforms experience into capability.

Pandemic Readiness and Vaccine Supply Coordination

Pandemics represent a fundamentally different category of challenge. They do not reflect incremental variations on seasonal patterns. They disrupt the very assumptions on which pharmacy operations are built. Supply chains fracture, demand spikes across unrelated categories simultaneously, workforce availability becomes uncertain, and public anxiety amplifies every shortage.

Pandemic readiness is an organisational capability, not a crisis response plan kept in a folder. It requires continuous attention, scenario thinking, and investment in resilience. It begins with acknowledging that perfect prediction is impossible. The objective of preparedness is not to foresee the specific crisis but to build flexibility and strength of response.

The first pillar of readiness is scenario planning. Leadership and operations teams should regularly review high-impact hypothetical situations, not to predict which will occur but to understand the implications of rapid change. What happens if supply contracts? If transportation slows? If staffing falls by one third? If documentation requirements change overnight? These discussions surface vulnerabilities long before they are exposed by reality.

Another foundational element is establishing a clear priority hierarchy for products. During pandemics, demand often outpaces supply across multiple fronts. Not all demand can be satisfied equally. Pharmacies must protect access to life-sustaining medicines, chronic therapies, and medically necessary preventive products first. Elective or comfort-oriented categories may be managed with greater flexibility. Establishing these priorities in advance reduces reactive decision-making under stress.

Vaccine management during pandemics introduces its own layer of complexity. Vaccines are tightly regulated, emotionally charged, and often limited in availability. Coordination with public health authorities, vaccine manufacturers, and accredited distributors is essential. Pharmacies need clear mechanisms for eligibility verification, allocation tracking, administration documentation, and follow-up scheduling.

Cold chain integrity becomes a non-negotiable operational domain. Vaccines demand specific storage conditions, constant temperature monitoring, validated equipment, and trained handling. Any breach in cold chain management can render doses unusable and represents both financial loss and missed public health opportunity. During pandemics, when vaccine supply is constrained, such losses are ethically and operationally unacceptable.

Communication around vaccines also needs careful calibration. Public expectations are shaped by government announcements, media narratives, and social discourse. Pharmacies must avoid overpromising or speculating on availability. Clear, factual communication about what is currently available, how appointments are scheduled, and what documentation is required reinforces credibility and reduces frustration.

Staff readiness during pandemics extends beyond clinical competence. Teams face sustained stress, fear of exposure, extended working hours, and emotionally charged interactions with anxious customers. Leadership must prioritise staff safety through provision of protective equipment, clear safety protocols, and emotional support. Burnout cannot be ignored. A workforce that feels protected performs better and demonstrates greater empathy.

Workforce continuity planning becomes critical. Supply of trained personnel may diminish due to illness, quarantine requirements, or travel restrictions. Cross-training, backup staffing pools, flexible scheduling, and remote support functions strengthen resilience. Centralised prescription review, remote counselling support, or call centre triage can relieve pressure on store personnel while maintaining service quality.

As pandemics recede, complacency becomes a risk. Hard-earned lessons fade quickly without intentional documentation and integration into organisational memory. Post-pandemic reviews should be conducted with the same seriousness as financial audits. What operational decisions worked? Where did bottlenecks occur? Which communication approaches reduced confusion? Which systems failed silently? Documenting these insights and updating SOPs converts crisis experience into institutional capacity.

Pharmacies that institutionalise learning emerge stronger. Those that treat pandemics as once-in-a-generation anomalies remain vulnerable the next time conditions change.

Stocking Strategies for Sudden Surges in Demand

Stocking strategies during sudden surges present one of the most intricate operational challenges. These situations test the dual obligations of serving community needs while maintaining discipline with capital, compliance, and fairness.

Stocking decisions must be grounded in visibility and data. Real-time inventory data across stores, warehouses, and transit allows leadership to identify pressure points as they emerge. Without accurate visibility, decisions are reactive, late, and often ineffective. Investment in reliable inventory systems is not a luxury. It is the backbone of surge management.

Historical patterns provide useful reference points but not certainty. Demand curves shift, new conditions emerge, community behavior changes. Historical analysis should be combined with real-time signals such as sudden uplift in search trends, supplier alerts on lead times, and field reports from store teams.

Clear classification of critical items sharpens focus. Life-sustaining medicines, essential symptom relief products, and preventive items should be protected first. Secondary categories can tolerate variability. A disciplined approach prevents dilution of focus and preserves access to essential products.

Decentralised decision-making within controlled boundaries improves responsiveness. Centralised control slows down reaction in dynamic circumstances. Allowing stores limited autonomy to reorder within predefined parameters allows them to respond to local conditions efficiently. Central oversight remains critical to prevent excess stock accumulation or inequitable distribution.

Supplier partnerships transform during surges. Long-term, respectful relationships tend to receive prioritisation from distributors under constrained supply. Chains that have established credibility through consistent payment practices, fair dealing, and transparent communication tend to fare better when supply tightens unexpectedly.

Quantity limits are sometimes necessary to prevent hoarding and misuse. Important items must be capped per customer to protect broader access. Clear signage, calm explanations, and consistent enforcement help customers understand that limits are in place to protect the community, not to withhold care.

Internal stock redistribution is a powerful, underused tool. Surplus inventory in lower-demand regions can be transferred to high-pressure areas provided logistics and processes allow quick movement. These decisions require logistical coordination, clear accounting, and rapid execution.

Exit planning must accompany surge entry planning. Demand surges eventually subside. Inventory levels stocked during high demand must be unwound thoughtfully. Redistribution, returns to suppliers, or controlled discounting reduce expiry risk and capital lock-in. Chains that plan only for entry into surges often face cluttered inventory and write-offs later.

Stocking strategies during emergencies reveal leadership character. Decisions made under pressure expose priorities. Pharmacies that prioritise access, fairness, and operational discipline earn lasting trust. Those that prioritise short-term gain erode long-term credibility.

Seasonal and emergency demand management is not a peripheral operational topic. It is a central expression of what a pharmacy chain stands for. These moments test systems, people, and values simultaneously. Demand surges reveal strengths and expose weaknesses. The public remembers how pharmacies behave in moments of need far more than in ordinary times.

Managing flu seasons and localized health spikes requires preparation, disciplined execution, clear communication, and ethical judgment.

Pandemic readiness requires adaptability, scenario thinking, coordination with external partners, and investment in resilience. Stocking strategies must balance realism with responsiveness, maintaining access without panic or waste.

The most dependable pharmacy chains accept uncertainty as part of the health landscape. Their objective is not perfect foresight but dependable response. Through disciplined planning, strong systems, principled leadership, and respect for human dignity, pharmacies can serve communities effectively when the need is greatest.

In a world where health risks evolve quickly and public anxiety spreads widely, the ability to manage demand under pressure is not only a professional advantage. It is a moral obligation and a foundational measure of institutional maturity and civic contribution.

References

- https://www.who.int/health-topics/influenza
- https://www.cdc.gov/flu/season/index.html
- https://www.who.int/initiatives/vaccine-safety-net
- https://www.cdc.gov/pharmaceuticalsafety/emergencypreparedness.html
- https://www.who.int/teams/integrated-health-services/patient-safety
- https://www.fip.org/emergencies
- https://www.who.int/teams/immunization-vaccines-and-biologicals
- https://www.unicef.org/supply/vaccines
- https://www.cdc.gov/vaccines/vpd/polio/index.html
- https://www.who.int/teams/health-product-policy-and-standards/
- https://www.who.int/initiatives/medical-product-regulatory-harmonization
- https://hbr.org/2021/02/a-guide-to-managing-your-supply-chain-risk

Chapter 14

Managing Expiry and Returns

Pharmacy inventory is fragile in two distinct senses. First, medicines are perishable: they have chemical lives that end at a date printed on the pack. Second, medicines are trust instruments: expired stock or mishandled returns damage reputation and can harm patients. Managing expiry and returns, therefore, matters for finance, for compliance, and for public safety. Done well, it preserves margin, protects patients, and reduces regulatory risk. Done badly it creates avoidable waste, triggers inspections, and erodes the core public purpose of a pharmacy.

This chapter examines how pharmacies should organise their day to day systems and strategic policies to manage expiry and returns with professionalism. We will cover inventory rotation methods and their practical application, approaches to handling short expiry stock and supplier returns, tactics to minimise financial loss from wastage, and the legal and environmental responsibilities that frame these activities. Each section aims to be operationally useful, not theoretical. Practical checklists, decision rules, and examples appear in the text so that managers can translate judgment into consistent action.

FIFO and FEFO Methods

Inventory rotation is the single most effective lever to reduce expiry losses. Two terms dominate the discussion: First In First Out, commonly known as FIFO, and First Expiry First Out, commonly known as FEFO. They look similar at a glance but are materially different in practice and in their relevance to medicines.

FIFO means you pull stock in the order you received it. It is intuitive and easy to implement. It works well for products where the receipt sequence generally aligns with expiry. In many retail contexts, FIFO reduces holding time and keeps stock flowing.

FEFO means you prioritise stock by earliest expiry date irrespective of when it was received. FEFO is the best practice for regulated medicines because manufactured batches arrive with variable shelf lives. Two batches of the same tablet may arrive on different dates with different expiry horizons. When medicines are subject to strict stability requirements, FEFO prevents slow moving batches with earlier expiry from being buried behind newer stock.

Good distribution practice guidelines and international pharmaceutical regulators explicitly favour FEFO for medicinal products because it is aligned to product safety. FEFO reduces the risk that consumers receive near expired or expired product and therefore is the preferred rotation strategy for pharmacies that manage a mixture of long and short dated SKUs.

Practical implementation depends on systems and layout. Manual rotation without software is possible but fragile. The simplest operational rule is to make expiry date visible at each pick face. This may mean repackaging products into transparent bins that clearly display month and year, or using prominent shelf tags with expiry dates. At the moment of receiving goods, the receiving clerk should affix a visible expiry sticker on each carton or tray so that pickers do not have to read tiny printed dates under time pressure.

Software helps. Modern inventory systems support FEFO rules natively. When an order is released to pick, the warehouse management system recommends the exact pallet or bin to pick from based on closest expiry. That reduces human judgment calls and prevents mistakes during busy shifts.

FEFO does not exist in a vacuum. A FEFO policy must be paired with receiving rules. When goods arrive, receiving must record both the batch number and the expiry precisely. Accept only correctly labelled cartons and document any discrepancies immediately with the supplier. Receipts into the system should block stock that arrives with short remaining shelf life unless there is an explicit management override and a planned action, such as immediate promotion or prearranged return.

A common exception arises with controlled temperature products. For cold chain items, rotation via FEFO must also account for storage location segmentation. You should never mix refrigerated stock of different expiry horizons in a way that makes picking by expiry impossible. Temperature controlled storage should be organised in clearly labelled bays with expiry visible.

There is a human factor in any rotation strategy. Even the best systems can fail if staff are not trained and audited. Routine floor audits are the hygiene that keeps rotation working. A short audit checklist for rotation might include the following items checked weekly: are near-expiry items fronted and clearly labelled, are expired items segregated into a locked quarantine location, does the system pick list match physical stock, and are rejects logged with photos and supplier communication documented. These audits should be short, sharp, and routine.

Finally, rotation strategy must be communicated to the whole store team. FEFO is not an inventory team technicality: it affects sales staff, pharmacists and store managers. If a sales associate places a newer box at the front because it looks nicer, an expiry loss follows. Make FEFO visible, make it simple, and measure adherence.

Handling Short-Expiry Medicines and Supplier Returns

Short-expiry medicines require deliberate handling from the moment of receipt. A batch with three months to expiry needs a different disposition than a batch with two years. The margin for error is small, and the correct actions are operational rather than theoretical.

Design a short-expiry policy and make it immutable. A pragmatic policy has graded steps tied to remaining shelf life. For example:

- More than 12 months to expiry: normal stock, full price.
- 6 to 12 months to expiry: monitor and consider targeted promotions in suitable outlets.
- 3 to 6 months to expiry: move to prominent "use soon" zones, offer to healthcare partners with clear labelling, consider internal transfers to higher throughput stores.
- Less than 3 months to expiry: quarantine and initiate return or destruction protocol as per supplier and regulatory rules.

The exact cutoffs depend on product category. Vaccines and biologicals usually require longer lead times and therefore demand stricter rules. Injectable solutions often cannot be discounted or redistributed easily and need early visibility on arrival.

Returns to suppliers are an operational art. Contracts must specify return windows, financial terms, and logistical expectations at the moment of onboarding vendors. Expectation mismatch is a major cause of contention later. A useful clause is a defined list of eligible return reasons that include expiry within a specified horizon at receipt, damaged packaging, incorrect product, or batch recalls. The financial terms should clarify whether the supplier will reimburse full cost, offer credit, or arrange destruction at their cost.

Do not treat returns as ad hoc. A returns process must be transactional and traceable. Each returned pallet or carton should have a return authorization number, accompanied by photocopies or scanned images of the receiving records showing the expiry dates. Capture photos of the physical item, the serials or barcodes, and the damage if any. Use a returns manifest that logs condition, reason code, and dispatch details. This creates a traceable chain of custody and reduces disputes with suppliers.

Supplier relationships change the dynamic of returns. Suppliers who treat returns seriously are often those with established quality systems and mature distribution. Build preferred vendor lists and negotiate service level agreements for returns. When suppliers are responsible for pick up, schedule collections and have internal staff ready to quarantine and hand over goods safely.

Where suppliers do not accept returns, you will need a planned disposition. For some products a manufacturer may instruct disposal through authorised waste handlers. For others you may be able to transfer to a clinical programme, for example donation to a government hospital or NGO where the expiry window matches immediate need and regulations permit donation. Document every action comprehensively and retain supplier correspondence.

Short expiry handling also requires commercial imagination. Controlled promotions targeted at high throughput outlets, bundling with complementary products, or temporary price adjustments can move stock fast without eroding perceived value if done transparently and sparingly. Avoid routine discounting as a default solution: overuse trains purchasing behaviour and increases future risk.

Finally, manage the pharmacy network flow. Transfers from low demand to high demand stores reduce national or regional expiry loss. For example, rural outlets with low turnover might send near-expiry inventory to urban clinics with higher patient throughput. This internal redistribution is often faster and cheaper than external returns and avoids destruction where product can still be used safely and legally.

Minimising Financial Losses Due to Wastage

Expiry losses are not only clinical problems. They are financial events that erode working capital and profitability. The most expensive expiry is the one you did not anticipate. Reducing wastage requires a multi layer approach: prevention, mitigation, and recovery.

Prevention begins with procurement discipline. Buy to forecast and keep safety stock calibrated to true variability, not gut feel. Use rolling forecasts that blend sales velocity, seasonality, promotion plans, and days in transit. Scenario based buffers reduce both stockouts and overstock. When a new product is introduced, start conservatively and let replenishment increase only after velocity stabilises.

Demand sensing improves procurement. Real time sales data, combined with external signals such as public health bulletins, search trends, and supplier lead time alerts, allows more responsive ordering. If cough syrup sales start accelerating in a cluster, trigger local replenishment rules before national averages catch up.

Mitigation is the set of actions you take as expiry risk approaches. Clear examples include:

- Shelf fronting for near-expiry stock to maximise visibility at point of sale.
- Targeted promotions to trusted customer segments, such as chronic patients who already use the product, but only when clinically appropriate.
- Transfers to higher throughput channels.
- Bundle offers with products that maintain clinical appropriateness.
- Coordination with NGOs or public health programmes for donation when permitted.

Recovery is what you do after loss occurs. This includes documented returns to suppliers, insurance claims if the loss is due to transport failure, or controlled destruction with cost allocation. Internal accounting should track expiry losses per store and per SKU to create accountability. When expiry loss is visible in performance dashboards, it becomes a management issue rather than accounting noise.

Cost allocation matters. If expiry is always charged to a generic expense pool, no one owns the problem. Instead, allocate expiry to the responsible cost centre: buying team for forecasting errors, store manager for mishandling stock, or logistics for transport failures. This creates specific improvement targets.

Build expiry KPIs into regular reviews. Useful metrics include expiry rate as percent of inventory value, number of SKUs with expiry within 90 days, and days of inventory per SKU. Benchmark stores by region and size and celebrate improvements. Operational change is achieved through measurement and behavioural incentives.

Insurance can help but is not a substitute for operational competence. Some losses are insurable, like documented temperature excursion during transport. Others, like obsolescence due to poor forecasting, are not. Understand what your policies cover and use insurance as last line protection, not the primary control.

Technology investments pay back in faster ways than most managers expect. Automated expiry alerts, push notifications when SKUs approach threshold age, and pick lists that direct FEFO picking reduce human error. Integrate these alerts into the daily opening checklist so that front line managers act early.

Finally, think about product lifecycle management. Some SKUs have short life because of changing guidelines or frequent label updates. If a product is prone to obsolescence, consider shorter order cycles, smaller order quantities, or exclusive special orders rather than stocking for all customers.

Legal and Environmental Considerations

Expiry and returns do not exist outside law and ecology. Pharmacies must operate inside the regulatory framework for pharmaceutical waste and consumer protection. The legal footprint differs by country, but three themes recur: mandated return responsibilities, the need for documented disposal, and environmental obligation.

In India, regulatory guidance clarifies responsibilities for expired or unused drugs and requires that these be returned to the supplier or manufacturer. The Central Drugs Standard Control Organization publishes guidance on disposal which spells out timelines for return and responsibilities for licensed entities. Retailers are required to follow these procedures, and documentation must be retained for inspection. Failure to follow the rules attracts penalties and reputational damage. (cdsco.gov.in)

Environmental law is increasingly active on pharmaceutical waste. Medicines should not be dumped in landfill or sewerage indiscriminately. Biomedical Waste Management Rules require proper segregation and disposal of pharmaceutical waste including expired products, especially injectables and cytotoxic materials. Central Pollution Control Boards and state agencies enforce these rules and have issued specific guidance on segregation, storage, and handover to authorised waste handlers. Non compliance can lead to fines, licence suspension, and community harm. (hspcb.org.in)

Document the whole chain of events. When returning to supplier, keep records of return authorisations, transport manifests, and supplier confirmations. When transferring to an authorised waste handler, obtain collection receipts and disposal certificates. Maintain digital copies for the statutory retention period and make them accessible to auditors.

Environmental responsibility is not only a legal obligation. It is brand capital. Customers increasingly view proper disposal as a marker of professionalism and care. Properly documented returns and an environmentally sound destruction record are defensive assets during inspections and marketing strengths during community outreach.

There are special regulations for controlled substances. Opioids and other narcotics require even stricter control in storage, return and destruction. In some jurisdictions the regulator prescribes destruction methods such as incineration under defined conditions. Work with authorised handlers and follow the chain of custody rules precisely.

Return and disposal also have safety implications inside the store. Expired medicines should be segregated in a locked quarantine area away from access. Do not allow expired stock to mix with sellable stock. Train staff to quarantine items immediately upon discovery and to place clear labels on quarantine containers with the reason and date. Avoid ad hoc disposal. A separate SOP for quarantine, evaluation, and disposition protects staff and patients.

When you use third party authorised waste handlers, perform vendor due diligence. Ensure that the handler is authorised by the relevant environmental authority, has secure transport protocols, and provides certificates of destruction. Periodically audit handlers and ask for GPS enabled manifests for high risk consignments.

Finally, consider environmental optimisation so expiry never becomes the only metric of success. Reducing single use packaging, ordering smaller lot sizes for fast changing lines, and engaging suppliers on takeback programs all reduce environmental pressure. Some suppliers run stewardship programmes to take back unused products for safe disposal; partnering with them reduces your burden and improves compliance.

Practical Checklist for Managers

To operationalise the chapter quickly, here is a compact checklist managers can apply weekly and monthly:

Weekly checklist

- Run expiry alert report and highlight SKUs with less than 120 days to expiry.
- Physically inspect top 20 SKUs by value and velocity for correct rotation.
- Move quarantined items to the secure returns area and generate return authorisations.
- Check FEFO and confirm pick faces show earliest expiry in front.
- Validate that returns manifests are correctly recorded and supplier communications logged.

Monthly checklist

- Reconcile system inventory with physical stock for 10 percent of SKUs.
- Run expiry loss KPI and allocate responsibility for anomalies.
- Review supplier contract terms on returns and penalties; seek improvements where needed.
- Audit authorised waste handler documentation and certificates of destruction.
- Hold a short postmortem on any significant expiry event and document corrective actions.

Expiry and returns are not minor back office chores. They are central operational disciplines that touch procurement, warehousing, pharmacy ethics, compliance, and brand reputation. The decisions a chain makes about rotation, about short expiry handling, and about supplier returns determine both margin and patient safety. Legal responsibilities and environmental stewardship create constraints but also opportunities to demonstrate professionalism.

FEFO backed by strong receiving discipline, visible shelf management, and software assistance reduces the most common cause of loss. Short expiry stock must be treated as a priority and governed by clear disposition rules. Minimising loss requires a combination of better forecasting, rapid mitigation, internal transfers, and contractual clarity with suppliers. Finally, compliance with disposal laws and engagement with authorised waste managers protect both public health and the business.

A pharmacy chain that manages expiry and returns well converts a vulnerable liability into a source of strength. It reduces cost, avoids inspection risk, and signals to the community that it treats medicines with the gravity they deserve.

References

- https://www.who.int/docs/default-source/medicines/norms-and-standards/guidelines/distribution/trs961-annex9-modelguidanceforstoragetransport.pdf
- https://www.fda.gov/drugs/pharmaceutical-quality-resources/expiration-dates-questions-and-answers
- https://www.fda.gov/inspections-compliance-enforcement-and-criminal-investigations/inspection-technical-guides/expiration-dating-and-stability-testing-human-drug-products
- https://cdsco.gov.in/opencms/resources/UploadCDSCOWeb/2018/UploadPublic_NoticesFiles/Guidance%20document%20on%20disposal.pdf
- https://www.who.int/publications/i/item/guidelines-for-safe-disposal-of-unwanted-pharmaceuticals-in-and-after-emergencies
- https://hspcb.org.in/uploads/laws/BMW_Rules.pdf
- https://cpcb.nic.in/uploads/projects/bio-medical-waste/guidelines_healthcare_june_2018.pdf
- https://www.gmp-compliance.org/gmp-news/fifo-fefo-lifo-what-is-the-meaning

- https://www.fda.gov.ph/wp-content/uploads/2021/03/World-Health-Organization-Good-Distribution-Practices.pdf
- https://www.netsuite.com/portal/resource/articles/inventory-management/reverse-logistics.shtml
- https://airpharm.com/en/blog/reverse-logistics-expired-pharmaceutical-products/
- https://www.pbahealth.com/elements/fifo-lifo-or-fefo-which-inventory-valuation-method-is-better-for-pharmacies/
- https://www.savinodelbene.com/fifo-fefo-what-they-are-how-they-work/

Chapter 15

Ethical Selling and Pharmacy Code of Conduct

Pharmacy is a commercial activity and a health profession at the same time. That dual identity creates constant tension. Selling is necessary for business survival. Caring is necessary for professional integrity and patient safety. Ethical selling is the art of honoring both obligations simultaneously. It protects patients, preserves trust, and makes long term business sense.

A pharmacy code of conduct is not a legal document alone. It is a compact between the business and the community. It explains how the pharmacy will act when incentives pull in different directions. At the counter, decisions are fast and human. The code of conduct turns abstract professional values into simple rules and operating instincts staff can act on under pressure.

This chapter examines three central domains of pharmacy ethics: avoiding cross selling abuses, respecting prescriptions, and counseling patients. Each area has operational implications that go beyond signage and training. They influence procurement, merchandising, performance measurement, incentives, and leadership. Ethical practice in these domains reduces harm, builds loyalty, and aligns commercial success with professional purpose.

Avoiding Cross-Selling Abuses

Cross selling is a familiar retail tool. It boosts average transaction value and may introduce customers to useful products they might not have considered. In pharmacies, cross selling becomes ethically fraught because the product being sold can affect health. A well chosen accessory, like a pill organizer, adds value. An aggressive push of antibiotics, cough suppressants, or unproven supplements crosses an ethical line.

Abuse of cross selling takes many forms. It can be overt, such as promotional placement that encourages purchase of prescription substitutes without clear explanation. It can be subtle, such as incentive schemes that reward staff financially for selling specific medicines or categories without clinical rationale. It can also be structural, such as merchandising decisions that place high margin health supplements directly beside prescription fills in a way that nudges anxious patients toward unnecessary purchases.

Business systems often create the incentives that lead to cross selling abuses. Commission schemes, sales contests, or bonus plans tied to category performance can distort judgment. The simplest response is to design incentives that align with patient outcomes rather than short term sales. Encourage adherence, high quality counselling, and accurate dispensing. Reward staff for low error rates, good documentation, and patient satisfaction scores rather than for pushing particular products.

Merchandising must be thoughtful. Avoid placing prescription class medicines, or their immediate alternatives, as impulse items near the counter. Non-prescription supportive items such as masks, thermometers, or moisturizing balm can be displayed in accessible ways, but anything likely to be used in place of clinical judgment needs a clear separation and a pharmacist cue for discussion.

Promotions must have rules. If a product is promoted, establish clinical suitability checks that pharmacists can use before applying the offer to a sale. For example, a discount on a cough syrup might be conditional on patient counselling about symptom duration and red flags, and the offer should not apply to antibiotics or other prescription-only medicines. Avoid promotional language that implies cure or superiority without evidence.

Design operational scripts that help staff move from impulse prompts to clinical checks. A cashier or assistant should be trained to say something simple like this when a customer reaches for a promoted medicine that could be inappropriate: "This product can help with mild coughs. If the cough has lasted more than a few days or if there is breathlessness, our pharmacist will review your condition before you buy." Simple language reduces impulse buying without moralizing the customer.

Monitor promotions and outcomes. If a promotional campaign drives returns, complaints, or adverse event reports, stop it and investigate. Keep records of promotion-related complaints and examine them in monthly governance reviews. This discipline prevents repeated mistakes and signals that ethics matter.

Online channels require special attention. Digital offers, pop-up suggestions, and cart-level nudges can be more persuasive than in-store displays because they reach customers when they are alone and anxious. Digital product recommendations should be filtered by prescription status. If a customer uploads a prescription, algorithms should not suggest alternatives that undermine prescriber intent. If a product requires pharmacist review, do not allow automated one-click purchase without an intervening clinical check.

Transparency is a core principle. If a promotion is manufacturer-sponsored or funded by a vendor, disclose it. The public has a right to understand commercial arrangements that influence availability or price. Many professional codes require disclosure of conflicts of interest for pharmacists. Make this disclosure routine.

Finally, leadership must model restraint. Strong codes of conduct are useless if leadership implicitly rewards the opposite behaviour.

Celebrate cases in which staff declined a sale because the pharmacy's professional responsibilities came first. Public recognition creates cultural norms more powerful than memos.

Respecting Prescriptions

A prescription is a clinical instruction from a trained prescriber. Respecting prescriptions is not about blind obedience. It is about professional stewardship. The pharmacist validates dosing, checks for interactions, ensures legal requirements are met, and clarifies ambiguous instructions. At each of these steps the pharmacist acts as a patient safety expert and a guardian of public health.

Respect begins with acceptance criteria. When a prescription arrives, the pharmacy must confirm the prescriber's details, the date, and the specific medicines and dosages. If a prescription is incomplete or illegible, the pharmacist has an obligation to clarify. That may require calling the prescriber, clarifying with the patient, or refusing to dispense until adequate information is available. In many regulatory frameworks, dispensing against a dubious prescription is a breach of professional duty.

Substitution policies are another critical area. Generic substitution, therapeutic interchange, or brand substitution have economic and public health dimensions. A pharmacy policy should define when substitution is acceptable, how consent is obtained from the patient, and how the substitution is documented. In many countries substitution of controlled drugs or narrow therapeutic index medicines is not permitted. Understand local rules and place them into the operational flow.

Document each substitution. Record the original prescription, the substituted product, batch and expiry, and the patient's consent. This record protects the pharmacy and supports continuity of care. If a patient later reports an adverse event, the documentation allows pharmacovigilance and clear communication with prescribers.

Handling Schedule H, H1 and X medicines requires particular care. These classes often require special registers, retention of prescription copies, and stricter storage. Ensure staff understand the paperwork requirements and that the physical security of scheduled products meets statutory standards. Regular audits must include checks for register completeness and the physical security of controlled products.

Refusal to dispense is sometimes necessary. If a prescription appears forged, or if the prescribing pattern indicates potential diversion, the pharmacist must act. Refusal should be handled with firmness and compassion. Explain the reason to the patient without accusation. Offer to contact the prescriber for verification or suggest a clinical review. Avoid confrontational language. Keep records of the incident and escalate to the appropriate authority when necessary.

E-prescriptions and digital workflows change the dynamics but not the duty. Verify digital prescriber identity when possible. Maintain secure storage and audit trails for digital prescriptions. When prescriptions arrive via teleconsult platforms, connect with the prescribing clinician if needed. Document verification steps so that audit trails reflect professional judgement.

Prescription respect also extends to privacy. Never share prescription details with third parties without patient consent. Data protection laws apply. Keep hard copy and electronic records secure. Train staff on minimal necessary access and the expectation of confidentiality. Privacy is a form of respect.

Finally, treat high risk situations as opportunities for proactive care. When a prescription includes polypharmacy, potentially interacting drugs, or high dose regimens, take a moment to counsel the patient, contact the prescriber if necessary, and consider medication reconciliation. Patients on multiple medications often benefit more from time and attention than from rapid throughput.

Counseling Patients

Counseling is where clinical competence meets human contact. A well counselled patient is safer, more likely to adhere, and more likely to trust the pharmacy. Yet counseling is often the first activity to be squeezed when footfall rises or targets loom. Ethical practice insists that counseling is non negotiable.

Effective counseling has a clear structure and a humane delivery. Start with the essentials. Confirm the patient's name and reason for the medicine. Explain what the medicine is for, how and when to take it, the expected timeline for benefit, and the most important side effects to watch for. Use plain language and avoid medical jargon.

Prioritise the truly important counselling points. Patients remember three things in a short interaction. Give them the three that matter most for safety: dose and timing; what to do about a missed dose; the most dangerous side effects and when to seek medical help. For complex regimens or high risk medicines, offer a written instruction sheet to take home.

Use teach back techniques to confirm understanding. Ask the patient to explain in their own words how they will take the medicine. This reveals misunderstandings that simple yes or no questions do not catch. If the patient struggles to explain, rephrase and simplify.

Cultural competence influences counseling quality. Understand common language preferences and literacy levels in the catchment. Use visual aids for people who struggle with reading. For elderly patients, involve caregivers when available and appropriate. For patients with chronic disease, link counseling to broader adherence plans, scheduled refills, and reminders.

Document counseling. A simple checkbox and short note in the patient record that counseling occurred, the topics covered, and any particular concerns noted creates continuity. If a patient later visits another provider, these notes aid clinical decisions.

Pharmacovigilance is an integral part of counseling. Inform patients how to report suspected adverse reactions and give them a simple pathway to contact the pharmacy for questions. If patients perceive the pharmacy as responsive after starting a new medicine, adherence tends to improve.

Time and space matter. Counselling should occur in a setting that preserves privacy. If the store layout makes privacy impossible, create a private counselling booth or a designated corner. Visible privacy signals encourage patients to ask sensitive questions.

Technology can amplify counseling at scale when used wisely. Telepharmacy, secure messaging, and scheduled pharmacist video calls offer follow up without requiring the patient to return in person. Use these tools for chronic disease check ins and post discharge counseling where appropriate. However, do not allow technology to replace the human moment for initial high risk medicines.

Staff training is an ongoing discipline. Senior pharmacists should coach juniors in the art of concise, clear counseling. Role play, recorded observations, and peer feedback are effective development tools. Include counseling skills in competency assessments and link quality scores to recognition rather than punishment.

Measure counseling outcomes. Use patient satisfaction surveys, refill adherence rates, and follow up call logs to assess counseling effectiveness. Recognise and reward pharmacists who achieve consistently high counseling impact. This shifts culture from throughput worship to patient centred performance.

Ethical dilemmas arise. A patient may request a medicine for off label use or press for antibiotics against standard protocols. Use counseling as a moment of care rather than conflict. Explain the clinical rationale and safety concerns. Offer alternatives for symptom relief where appropriate. If a patient insists, document the interaction, seek prescriber input, and, if needed, refuse to dispense in a firm but compassionate way.

Finally, counseling must be accessible. Opening hours, language support, and affordability influence whether patients receive counseling at all. Design services that reach those who need them most: older adults, low literacy populations, and patients with complex regimens. Community outreach programmes, medication review clinics, and home visit models extend counselling reach well beyond the counter.

Making Ethics Operational

A code of conduct is effective only when embedded into everyday operations. Translate principles into simple rules and processes. Examples include:

- No commission on prescription medicines. Remove financial incentives from clinical decisions.
- Mandatory counseling for specific classes of medicines. Document counseling and make it auditable.
- A written substitution policy with signed patient consent.
- Limits on promotions for high risk categories and a sign off process for any promotional campaign.
- A refusal protocol including documentation, patient explanation script, and escalation path.
- Training and competency checks for all staff on ethical practice and privacy.
- Transparent disclosure of commercial relationships and sponsored promotions.
- Governance reviews that report ethical incidents to leadership monthly and publicly summarise corrective actions.

Ethics needs enforcement and reinforcement. Use audits, mystery shopping, complaint analysis, and staff interviews to monitor adherence. Make ethical performance part of appraisal and promotion decisions.

Leadership must be unambiguous. Public statements that the pharmacy values patient safety over short term margins are small acts that orient culture. More powerful is consistent practice: disallowing promotions that create clinical risk, refusing supplier pressure to compromise on documentation, and protecting staff who decline unethical requests.

Community engagement builds reputational capital. Host health education sessions, open medicine disposal days, and support local public health clinics. When the community sees consistent care, commercial success becomes a byproduct of trust rather than its driver.

Ethical selling and a strong code of conduct are not soft ideals. They are practical foundations of sustainable pharmacy practice. They protect patients, reduce legal exposure, and build the kind of trust that generates resilient revenue.

Avoid abuses by aligning incentives with patient wellbeing. Treat prescriptions as clinical documents that require respect, verification, and documentation. Counsel patients with compassion, clarity, and skill. Translate principles into processes that are simple to train, easy to audit, and difficult to game.

Pharmacy is a daily interface of commerce and care. Every interaction matters. The cumulative effect of responsible choices is a reputation that patients and prescribers prefer, regulators respect, and communities rely on. That is the commercial payoff and the moral dividend of ethical practice.

References

- https://www.who.int/docs/default-source/medicines/norms-and-standards/guidelines/distribution/trs961-annex8-fipwhoguidelinesgoodpharmacypractice.pdf

- https://www.fip.org/file/1586
- https://apps.who.int/iris/bitstream/handle/10665/38125/924154239X_eng.pdf
- https://ipapharma.org/wp-content/uploads/2019/02/gpp-manua-1.pdf
- https://appharmacycouncil.gov.in/site/oath
- https://www.who.int/medicines/areas/rational_use/en/
- https://www.ismp.org/resources
- https://www.cdc.gov/medicationsafety/pharmacists.html
- https://www.who.int/publications/i/item/9789241500748
- https://www.who.int/ethics/publications/public_health_messaging/en/
- https://www.ncbi.nlm.nih.gov/pmc/articles/PMC10748552/
- https://www.ncbi.nlm.nih.gov/pmc/articles/PMC5409993/
- https://iris.who.int/handle/10665/164501

Bonus Resources

This section is designed to translate ideas into action. While the earlier chapters explore strategy, ethics, operations, and growth, the bonus resources focus on execution. These tools reflect practices observed across successful pharmacy businesses and are intended to serve as reference material for founders, operators, managers, and teams working on the ground.

The appendices that follow are not meant to be prescriptive in every context. They are starting points. Each pharmacy, chain, or organization should adapt them based on local regulations, scale, and operational realities. Used thoughtfully, these resources can save time, reduce errors, and support consistency across teams and locations.

Appendix A: Checklists

Checklists are often underestimated in professional environments. In pharmacy operations, they serve a critical purpose. They reduce reliance on memory, standardize execution, and ensure that essential steps are not skipped during busy or transitional periods. The following checklists reflect practical realities rather than ideal conditions.

Store Launch Checklist

Launching a pharmacy store is a complex exercise involving regulatory approvals, supply chain readiness, staffing, and customer trust. A rushed or incomplete launch often creates problems that persist for months.

A robust store launch checklist typically covers the following areas:

Regulatory and Compliance Readiness

- Valid drug license issued and displayed
- Pharmacist registration verified and on-site
- Local trade licenses and statutory approvals completed
- Schedule H, H1, and X compliance systems in place
- Fire safety and basic infrastructure approvals obtained

Infrastructure and Equipment

- Shelving, storage, and counters installed as per layout plan
- Refrigeration units installed, calibrated, and temperature logs initiated

- Power backup and internet connectivity tested
- POS systems installed and synced with inventory software
- CCTV and basic security measures operational

Inventory and Supply Chain

- Opening stock aligned with local demand profile
- Fast-moving and chronic medicines adequately stocked
- Expiry dates verified for all opening inventory
- Supplier invoices and batch details recorded
- Cold-chain items verified at receipt

Staffing and Training

- Pharmacist and support staff appointed
- Basic SOP training completed
- Emergency procedures explained
- Customer interaction and billing process rehearsed

Pre-Opening Validation

- Trial billing conducted
- Inventory reconciliation tested
- Mock customer interactions performed
- Documentation and registers reviewed

A structured launch checklist reduces post-opening chaos and signals professionalism from day one.

Staff Onboarding Checklist

Staff quality defines pharmacy quality. A strong onboarding process helps new employees understand expectations, responsibilities, and culture from the start.

An effective onboarding checklist includes:

Documentation and Verification

- Identity and qualification verification
- Pharmacist registration validation where applicable
- Employment documentation completed
- Confidentiality and ethics acknowledgment signed

Role and Responsibility Clarity

- Job responsibilities explained
- Reporting structure clarified
- Shift timings and attendance expectations communicated

Operational Training

- SOP overview provided
- Inventory handling and billing training completed
- Prescription handling and escalation rules explained
- Hygiene, safety, and emergency protocols covered

Ethics and Conduct

- Code of conduct discussed
- Prescription integrity emphasized
- Customer confidentiality explained
- Escalation process for ethical concerns clarified

Initial Evaluation

- Shadowing period completed
- Basic competency validated
- Feedback session conducted

Onboarding is not an event. It is a process that sets the tone for accountability and professionalism.

SOP Templates

Standard Operating Procedures bring predictability to complex operations. SOP templates act as reference points and training tools.

Typical SOP templates included in a pharmacy environment are:

- Store opening and closing procedures
- Prescription receiving and dispensing
- Inventory receiving, storage, and rotation
- Expiry identification and quarantine
- Handling Schedule H, H1, and X medicines
- Customer complaints and incident reporting
- Cold-chain management
- Audit and inspection readiness

SOPs should be written in simple language, reviewed periodically, and reinforced through training rather than stored unread.

Appendix B: Sample Forms and Templates

Documentation protects both patients and businesses. Standardized forms reduce ambiguity, improve traceability, and support compliance during audits or inspections.

Prescription Log Template

A prescription log helps maintain accountability and regulatory compliance.

Key elements typically include:

- Date of dispensing
- Prescription number
- Prescriber details
- Patient identifier
- Medicine name and strength
- Quantity dispensed
- Pharmacist signature
- Special category marker for regulated schedules

A well-maintained prescription log is often the first document reviewed during inspections.

Audit Checklist

Internal audits identify gaps before regulators do.

A practical audit checklist may include:

- License validity and display
- Pharmacist presence records
- Prescription documentation accuracy
- Inventory reconciliation
- Expiry and damaged stock handling
- Cold-chain temperature logs
- SOP adherence
- Customer complaint records

Regular audits reinforce discipline and reduce inspection anxiety.

Vendor Agreement Draft

Vendor relationships shape inventory quality and financial stability.

A basic vendor agreement should clearly define:

- Product quality standards
- Batch and expiry requirements
- Delivery timelines
- Return and replacement terms
- Credit periods
- Documentation expectations
- Dispute resolution mechanism

Clear agreements prevent misunderstandings and support long-term partnerships.

Acknowledgments

This book draws its strength from lived experience and collective wisdom. It would not have been possible without the pharmacists who show up every day behind counters, often unnoticed, yet deeply essential. Their patience, integrity, and resilience form the backbone of India's healthcare access.

We acknowledge the retailers and entrepreneurs who shared their journeys openly, including their missteps and learnings. Their willingness to reflect honestly enriched this work beyond theory.

We also acknowledge industry professionals, supply chain partners, regulators, and healthcare workers who continue to engage with complexity rather than avoid it. Their commitment to improving systems quietly, without spotlight, deserves recognition. Finally, gratitude is owed to the readers. By engaging with this subject thoughtfully, you contribute to a more informed and responsible healthcare ecosystem.

About the Author

This book is authored by Sujit Paul deeply engaged with India's pharmacy and healthcare retail ecosystem. The perspective presented here is shaped by years of hands-on involvement across operations, strategy, compliance, and growth.

The work reflects close engagement with pharmacy retailers, chains, distributors, healthcare startups, and industry stakeholders. It combines ground-level realities with strategic insight, informed by observation rather than abstraction.

The intent behind this book is not to prescribe one model, but to encourage thoughtful decision-making. Pharmacy retail in India is diverse by design. Its future depends on leaders who understand both responsibility and opportunity.

As the sector continues to evolve, the hope is that this book serves not only as a guide, but as a conversation starter among those building the next chapter of Indian healthcare access.

www.ingramcontent.com/pod-product-compliance
Lightning Source LLC
LaVergne TN
LVHW022215200926
848481LV00006B/1971
9798905604591